What's Wrong with Modern Money Theory?

Gerald A. Epstein

What's Wrong with Modern Money Theory?

A Policy Critique

palgrave
macmillan

Gerald A. Epstein
University of Massachusetts
Amherst, MA, USA

ISBN 978-3-030-26503-8   ISBN 978-3-030-26504-5 (eBook)
https://doi.org/10.1007/978-3-030-26504-5

© The Editor(s) (if applicable) and The Author(s), under exclusive license to Springer Nature Switzerland AG, part of Springer Nature 2019
This work is subject to copyright. All rights are solely and exclusively licensed by the Publisher, whether the whole or part of the material is concerned, specifically the rights of translation, reprinting, reuse of illustrations, recitation, broadcasting, reproduction on microfilms or in any other physical way, and transmission or information storage and retrieval, electronic adaptation, computer software, or by similar or dissimilar methodology now known or hereafter developed.
The use of general descriptive names, registered names, trademarks, service marks, etc. in this publication does not imply, even in the absence of a specific statement, that such names are exempt from the relevant protective laws and regulations and therefore free for general use.
The publisher, the authors and the editors are safe to assume that the advice and information in this book are believed to be true and accurate at the date of publication. Neither the publisher nor the authors or the editors give a warranty, expressed or implied, with respect to the material contained herein or for any errors or omissions that may have been made. The publisher remains neutral with regard to jurisdictional claims in published maps and institutional affiliations.

This Palgrave Pivot imprint is published by the registered company Springer Nature Switzerland AG
The registered company address is: Gewerbestrasse 11, 6330 Cham, Switzerland

To my PERI colleagues and students and their commitment to rigorous policy-relevant research and activism

Acknowledgements

This short book grew out of years of trying to understand what Modern Money Theory was saying. So when Anne Davis asked me if I wanted to write a paper for a panel at the Eastern Economic Associations and appear on a panel with Randy Wray on the topic of MMT, I decided it was time to take the plunge and finally put down on paper what I thought of it. This book is an outgrowth of that paper and discussions that followed from it.

I first want to thank my friend and colleague Bob Pollin with whom I have had many discussions over the years about MMT and who encouraged me to undertake this project. I also am greatly indebted to Esra Nur Uğurlu for excellent research assistance throughout the project. Without her insight and hard work, I could never have finished this book.

I have also received valuable comments from many colleagues and students. I would like to thank Adam Aboobaker, Michael Ash, Dean Baker, Tom Ferguson, Ilene Grabel, Marc Lavoie, Robert McCauley, Perry Mehrling, Tom Palley, Juan Antonio Montecino, and Robert Pollin for helpful comments on an earlier draft.

I also thank Aaron Medlin, a Ph.D. student at UMass Amherst who, on a completely volunteer basis, wrote an extensive annotated bibliography of MMT writings and arguments that relate to the claims of my Eastern Economic Association Paper and therefore this book. Although Aaron did not convince me of all his views on MMT, he certainly opened my eyes to a great deal of MMT work germane to this book. I am very grateful to Aaron for his efforts and for the spirit in which he undertook them.

More generally, of course, none of these people are responsible for any of the views I present here.

Finally, I thank my editor at Palgrave Macmillan, Elizabeth Graber, and her editorial assistant, Sophia Siegler, for their support and excellent work in shepherding this book through the publication process.

Contents

1 Introduction: Strange Bedfellows and the Rise of Modern Money Theory — 1

2 MMT Basics and the Sustainability of Money Financed Deficits — 17

3 Institutional Specificity and the Limited Policy Relevance of Modern Money Theory — 35

4 The Role of the Dollar as an International Currency and Its Limits in a Multi-Key Currency World — 45

5 "America First" Monetary Policy and Its Costs — 57

6 The Mystery of the Missing Minsky: Financial Instability as a Constraint on MMT Macroeconomic Policy — 65

7 An MMT Free Lunch Mirage Can Lead to Perverse Outcomes: Fight Your Friends, Spare Your Enemies — 77

8 Conclusion: Contours of a Progressive
   Macroeconomic Policy   89

Index   99

About the Author

Gerald A. Epstein is Professor of Economics and a founding Co-Director of the Political Economy Research Institute (PERI) at the University of Massachusetts, Amherst, USA. Epstein has written articles on numerous topics including financial crisis and regulation, alternative approaches to central banking for employment generation and poverty reduction, capital account regulations and the political economy of central banking and financial institutions. Epstein has worked with numerous UN agencies including the ILO, UNDESA, UNDP, and UNCTAD on the topics of macroeconomics and monetary policy in developing countries. His most recent volumes are: *The Handbook of the Political Economy of Financial Crises*, (co-edited with Martin Wolfson) and *The Political Economy of Central Banking: Contested Control and the Power of Finance*. In recent years he has been the recipient of two INET grants, one to study the "social efficiency" of the financial system and a second to look at the distributional impacts of quantitative easing. He has also won the Samuel F. Conti Faculty Fellowship Award from the University of Massachusetts, Amherst.

CHAPTER 1

Introduction: Strange Bedfellows and the Rise of Modern Money Theory

Abstract Modern Money Theory (MMT) has attracted a great deal of attention and a large number of adherents in recent years. Also sometimes called Modern Monetary Theory, the doctrine's appeal has largely come from its argument that governments that issue their own sovereign currencies do not have to pay for government expenditures—their central banks can simply create money. Mainstream and heterodox critiques have questioned the theoretical bases and the practical viability of this program. This chapter introduces my critique of these policy proposals based on their limited applicability, their possible dangers for developing countries, the advocates lack of attention to empirical evidence, and the dangerous political message it sends to progressives, among other problems.

Keywords Modern Money Theory · Post-Keynesian · Sovereign currency

1.1 INTRODUCTION

Modern Money Theory (MMT) has recently gained a significant amount of attention. From occupying a marginal corner of the marginalized "Post-Keynesian" economics five years ago or less, MMT has now drawn attention, support, and disdain from Wall Street speculators, Harvard economists Kenneth Rogoff and Lawrence Summers and even Jerome

Powell, the Chair of the Federal Reserve. Glossy profiles of some of MMT's most outspoken advocates, especially Ph.D. Economist Stephanie Kelton, have hit the internet (see for example Zach Carter's slightly over the top *"Stephanie Kelton Has the Biggest Idea In Washington; Once an outsider, her radical economic thinking won over Wall Street. Now she's changing the Democratic Party."*). Much of this new-found fame (and infamy) have stemmed from the positive views of MMT expressed by prominent progressive politicians, including Senator Bernie Sanders and Congresswoman Alexandria Ocasio-Cortez (AOC).[1]

The recent appeal of MMT is understandable. For almost forty years, neo-liberal economic theory and policy has dominated macroeconomic policy with its focus on balanced budgets, austerity and the elevation of "independent central banks" to focus on inflation to the virtual exclusion of all other goals, including full employment—(e.g., Epstein and Yeldan 2009; Pollin 2003). In this world, mainstream (neo-liberal) economics was used as a justification for macroeconomic policies that tolerated high unemployment, and government budgets that starved important public investments and social programs for the poor and working class. Mainstream Democrats in the US and similar politicians in Europe and elsewhere also adopted this approach, with devastating results on our economies and the livelihoods of many people (Blyth 2013). Austerity for the working class and riches for the rich also helped to fuel the rise of the populist right and authoritarianism in the US, Europe, and elsewhere.

The apex, and partial denouement of this neo-liberal austerity approach came with the onset of the Great Financial Crisis of 2007–2008 and the restoration of austerity budgets in Europe and to some extent in the US, following a brief post-meltdown "Keynesian" moment. Many people in the US and elsewhere could see the hypocrisy and venality of bail-outs for the bankers and austerity for everyone else. The pushback gained force with the devastating revelations of the problematic econometric analysis of Reinhart and Rogoff (2010) published by Herndon, Ash, and Pollin which greatly undermined the pseudo "scientific" underpinnings of the austerity

---

[1] For MMT's recent popularity among some progressive politicians, see Guida (2019) and Holland and Bosesler (2019). Among the recent well-known mainstream economic critics are Lawrence Summers, 2019, Fed Chair, Jerome Powell (McCormick 2019) and Rogoff (2019). Doug Henwood has recently criticized MMT from the left (Henwood 2019) while James Galbraith has come to MMT's defense (Galbraith 2019). For important contributions to the earlier, more academic, theoretical debates, see Mehrling (2000), Palley (2015a, b, 2019a, b), and Lavoie (2013). Wray (2012), is a classic presentation and defense of MMT.

ideology (Herndon et al. 2014). Yet, most Democratic politicians, including Barack Obama, Hillary Clinton, and Joe Biden, and their mainstream economists like Larry Summers, Tim Geithner, and Kenneth Rogoff continued to emphasize the dangers of government deficits and government debt at all times other than deep recessions.

MMT advocates questioned this austerity focus forcefully and developed an economic perspective to challenge it that was very attractive to those who saw the wrong-headedness and destructive nature of this mainstream economics and Democratic party embrace of austerity in the face of worsening income distribution, slow economic growth, and high unemployment.

In fact, the Republican Party had long ago abandoned the economics and practice of austerity economics—except for when Democrats were in power. Arthur Laffer, author of "supply-side economics," showed the Republicans that they could cut taxes for the rich and continue to feed the military-industrial complex and favored industries like Wall Street and big oil without tears or fears of deficits. Despite whole libraries of economic analysis discrediting the theory, Trump recently gave Laffer the Presidential Medal of Freedom for his service (to the Republican Party, that is):

"Arthur B. Laffer, the 'Father of Supply-Side Economics,' is one of the most influential economists in American history. He is renowned for his economic theory, the 'Laffer Curve,' which establishes the strong incentive effects of lower tax rates that spur investment, production, jobs, wages, economic growth, and tax compliance." Donald J. Trump, June 19, 2019[2] (see Waldman 2019).

This award comes on the heels of the massive Republican tax cuts of January 2019 for which Republican advocates variously claimed that supply-side impacts would mean there would be no increase in deficits and "no one cares about deficits anymore." MMT fits quite naturally into this space. Steve Englander refers to "a conservative version of modern monetary theory." "The conservative version sounds like the Fed-accommodated tax cut regime the Trump Administration seems to be supporting" (Englander 2019). Along these lines, in the summer of 2019 the *Washington Post* reports that Trump Chief Economist "Larry Kudlow dismisses deficit concerns as GOP abandons fiscal toughness" (Newmeyer 2019, *Washington Post*, June 14).

---

[2] https://www.whitehouse.gov/briefings-statements/president-donald-j-trump-award-medal-freedom/.

Meanwhile, after the initial counter crisis spending, Democrats and their mainstream economists continued to focus on limiting the budget deficits and the government debt accumulation despite relatively high unemployment, unmet social and economic needs, and a slowly growing economy.

In the face of this Democratic and their mainstream economics' focus on austerity and the dangers of deficits (except for during major recessions), MMT theorists were saying to anyone who would listen that government deficits were irrelevant, that austerity was costly and unnecessary and that the hapless Democrats and their economists were deathly wrong.

Yet, MMT theorists were not the first or only economists to criticize neo-liberal austerity economics. Orthodox Keynesian and heterodox economists more generally have been pushing back against this cynical and destructive policy and ideology for decades (see the articles, for example in Dymski et al. 1993; Palley 2015a, b; Blyth 2013; Galbraith 2012).[3]

For decades, most of my heterodox colleagues and I wrote and taught our students about the need for socially productive investments by the government; how we not only leave debts to future generations but also real assets from public investments. These public investments and full employment driven by sensible macroeconomic policy was the best policy for social good.

Other heterodox economists demonstrated empirically the folly of austerity economics. And while the Herndon, Ash, and Pollin critique of empirical claims by Rogoff and Reinhart "fiscal cliff" warnings received a great deal of attention and probably helped to break the global march toward more austerity, it is MMT, not other schools of post-Keynesian thought, that has recently received so much attention.[4]

A key reason that MMT has gained many adherents is that it puts this anti-austerity argument on a whole new plane. MMT claims that, in prin-

---

[3] I use the term "orthodox Keynesians" here to refer to economists who actually read and tried to implement Keynesian ideas, as opposed to the neo-Keynesians like Hicks, Samuelson, Solow, Tobin, Summers and others who adhered to a neo-classical version of Keynesianism. Joan Robinson referred to their economics as "Bastard Keynesianism" (Robinson 1974; see Crotty 2019 for a brilliant analysis of Keynes' economics).

[4] Very recently, a key bloc of former mainstream Democratic economist budget hawks in both the Clinton and Obama administrations, have begun to argue for a "new approach" to fiscal policy which is, for the most part, an implicit acknowledgement that the post-Keynesian and heterodox economists have been right about these issues (though they would not admit as much) (Blanchard and Summers 2017; Blanchard 2019; Furman 2016). I will discuss these ideas further below.

ciple, government spending never has to be paid for and is typically implemented by a mere stroke of the monetary pen. For them, we don't need to ask of progressive advocates for a "Green New Deal" or "Medicare for All": how are you going to pay for it? For MMTers, this question is not only unnecessary, but is also nonsensical (see, for example, Kelton, February 2, 2019). This way, MMT has recently been able to capture a large amount of attention in the progressive debate.

Roughly speaking, as developed by Randall Wray, Stephanie Kelton, and others, MMT's macroeconomic approach amounts to Abba Lerner's "functional finance" approach with a twist of "sovereign money" and "debt monetization" (Lerner 1943), based on the financial accounting of Wynne Godley (see Taylor 2008, for a discussion of Godley's contributions).[5] For them, the main goal of fiscal and monetary policy is to maintain full employment without (excessive) inflation. Their point about sovereign money is that governments do not need to save or levy taxes to "pay for" goods and services because all they need to do is print their sovereign currencies and use this money to acquire them. In fact, when the central bank and the treasury are institutionally connected, this money payment happens automatically, according to MMT. But, in the case of the US, and other countries, as Lavoie (2013) points out, these policies are not automatic, but amount to deliberate decisions by the Federal Reserve to monetize Treasury debt since the Federal Reserve charter prohibits the Fed from directly lending to the US government.

What then is the role of monetary and fiscal policy? There are two sides to this question. When the economy is operating below full employment/full capacity utilization, fiscal, and monetary policy should be used to increase aggregate demand to reach the full employment target. On the other hand, when the economy is running beyond full capacity, the "functional finance" claim is that the role of "taxes" and "borrowing" should be to drain spending from the economy when necessary to prevent excessive inflation, not to "finance" spending, per se.

A quote from Abba Lerner, the father of "functional finance" is instructive here:

---

[5] Wray and other MMT theorists say that their main influence is Hyman Minsky, not Abba Lerner. To be sure, Wray and others have written extensively about Minsky and his work is important for them. But, as I argue later, there seems to be little relationship between Minsky's work on credit, financial cycles and the need for financial regulations and MMT's macroeconomic policy analysis. This is an important issue that I address below.

In brief, Functional Finance rejects completely the traditional doctrines of "sound finance" and the principle of trying to balance the budget over a solar year or any other arbitrary period. In their place it prescribes: first, the adjustment of total spending (by everybody in the economy, including the government) in order to *eliminate both unemployment and inflation, using government spending when total spending is too low and taxation when total spending is too high*... (1943, 41)

MMT advocates often add that the proper target of monetary policy should be to keep interest rates very low in the long run, while fiscal policy should be adjusted when necessary to maintain full employment and moderate inflation (see, for example, Tymoigne 2009). According to MMT, any level of sovereign debt is sustainable in the narrow sense that the issuers of sovereign money will never need to default on its debt; they just need to print more money to service and even repay the debt if necessary.

The appeal of MMT theory to advocates of more government spending for progressive policies is therefore very understandable. Centered at the University of Missouri at Kansas and the Levy Institute and armed with a small army of MMT bloggers and advocates MMT began to slowly build up a small army of vociferous advocates (see Henwood 2019 for a description). Prominent among these blogs is that of Bill Mitchell (http://bilbo.economicoutlook.net/blog/) and New Economic Perspectives (http://neweconomicperspectives.org/), edited by legal scholar William Black. This "movement" spawned several networks of students who have organized conferences on MMT, mostly in the US. Most of these are connected to "liberal" or "progressive economic perspectives."

1.2 Strange Bedfellows

But, what is surprising is that some of the strongest advocates and supporters of MMT are not liberals or progressives, at all but are hedge fund operators, investors on Wall Street and libertarians. Warren Mosler, a hedge fund operator living in the Virgin Islands, has been a long time, generous supporter. He calls himself a "democratic member of the Tea Party," being a libertarian and an advocate of small government. In a piece published in Huffington Post, where Mosler expresses his disappointment with the Tea Party's stance on the idea of balanced budgets,[6] Mosler states that "...I

---

[6] https://www.huffpost.com/entry/tea-partys-economic-agend_b_700013.

have been, and continue to be, a strong supporter of the core Tea Party values of lower taxes, limited government, competitive market solutions, and a return to personal responsibility."

Mosler's networks in the financial world helped to spread MMT ideas to big finance (Carter 2018). For example, a number of bond traders and investment advisors have expressed interest in MMT (see, for example, the talks at this MMT conference https://www.youtube.com/watch?v= N8FhDsuJnvk). Even Ray Dalio, the billionaire founder of Bridgewater Associates, one of the world's largest investment companies, has written favorably about MMT (https://www.linkedin.com/pulse/its-time-look-more-carefully-monetary-policy-3-mp3-modern-ray-dalio/).

What can explain this confluence of strange bedfellows—progressive and socialist politicians like Senator Bernie Sanders and Alexandria Ocasio-Cortez and libertarians and hedge fund managers like Warren Mosler and Ray Dalio?

The financiers themselves have said that MMT helps them understand the movements of interest rates and inflation and the impact of monetary policies and budget deficits on these variables (see, for example, Parenteau, https://twitter.com/MacroEdge1 and investors speaking at the conference on MMT and Real World Financial Market Practitioners). Understandably, given their full employment, pre-Keynesian models, mainstream macroeconomics has failed to predict the course of inflation and interest rates. Investors and financial practitioners, now, as in the past, have embraced Keynesian and post-Keynesian ideas to understand the real workings of financial markets. This was true for example of the early Keynesians at the Federal Reserve Board and Federal Reserve Bank of New York during the Great Depression (Vernengo 2016), the credit focused Wall Street economists such as Albert Wojnilower in the 1970s and 1980s for whom both "monetarist" and "neo-Keynesian" economic theory was useless for understanding recent financial events.

In short, operatives in finance, both at the Fed and on Wall Street have almost always found the mainstream approaches wanting and have looked for other perspectives, especially Keynesian and post-Keynesian inspired ones. Some of these have clearly landed on the MMT branch of this group of economic theories.

But there are other reasons why MMT, among Post-Keynesian perspectives, might be most appealing to hedge fund managers and libertarians. It might also have to do with MMT scholars' long-standing efforts to popularize their ideas within the "financial community." Zach Carter of Huffington Post and Doug Henwood, financial journalist, have both described some of these efforts (Carter 2018; Henwood 2019). Carter argues that MMT built credibility by "circulating through the cocktail parties, expense-account dinners and conference rooms of high finance." Accordingly, Mosler used his friendships with people like Maurice Samuels, from Harvard Management Company, and Andres Drobny, professor of economics and a proprietary trader, to find avenues for MMT scholars. "In 2003, Mosler convinced Andres Drobny to host a dinner, exclusive to wealthy and eccentric figures from Wall Street, to which Stephanie Kelton would be invited to give a speech on MMT. At this dinner, Drobny invited Kelton to a small select conference he was hosting. Kelton's engagement with Drobny has introduced her to some of the elite networks that she has been using quite successfully to build her social credentials."

Perhaps the best example of the attempt to appeal to this group can be found in Stephanie Kelton's Bloomberg piece entitled: "*The Wealthy are Victims of Their Own Propaganda. To Escape Higher Taxes, They Must Embrace Deficits.*" In this article, Kelton claims rich people can avoid higher taxes if they adopt MMT thinking and see that deficits are not harmful, and that the government does not need taxes to pay for government spending: the Fed just needs to flick its monetary pen. She says that the rich should agree with MMT that, when it comes to government spending, we should stop asking the question of "who's going to pay for it?." Kelton praises MMT claiming that it can make both the poor and the rich, better off.

"Free lunchism" is, perhaps, what makes for these strange bedfellows. Progressives are led to believe that they don't have to be subject to the oppressive austerity theories and policies of mainstream Democratic politicians and their economists, and financiers believe that in a world guided by MMT, they can speculate and profit from virtually interest free credit, and no one is going to bother them to pay taxes since taxes are not needed to "pay for" government spending.

In trying to understand the policies emphasized—and the silence on other policies—keeping in mind this strange bedfellow mobilization by MMT advocates may be helpful. MMT policy advocates speak little about taxes and even deride the idea of raising progressive taxes. As I show in later chapters, despite the fact that some MMT associated economists, like William Black, and even Randall Wray write in other contexts about financial regulation, in the context of their core macro-policy work, they rarely mention Wall Street regulations as an important component of their macroeconomic policies, even though they are likely to be crucial in preventing a long-term low interest rate policy from leading to asset bubbles and financial crises. When they do, they focus on only regulating banks, and leave the massive and rapidly growing "shadow banking" network of hedge funds and asset managers out of the story completely. With very few exceptions, they write very little about the need for developing countries to implement capital controls to facilitate the full employment MMT policies they advocate. MMT's relative silence on these very Keynesian and Minskian-inspired policies might have something to do with their campaign to build bridges to hedge funds and other similar investors on Wall Street. I explore these questions in Chapter 6.

1.3 What This Book Does

Naturally, along with this positive attention, MMT has come in for a good deal of criticism. Some of it has been politically motivated. Five Republican Senators (all of whom voted for the massive, deficit creating Republican tax cuts of 2019) in an evident swipe against Bernie Sanders and Alexandria Ocasio Cortez submitted a resolution "Recognizing the duty of the Senate to condemn Modern Monetary Theory and recognizing that the implementation of Modern Monetary Theory would lead to higher deficits and higher inflation" (see US Senate, https://www.perdue.senate.gov/imo/media/doc/MMT%20Resolution.pdf).

But some has come from economists including from prominent heterodox economics.[7]

In fact, there has been a debate for more than a decade between MMT theorists and some heterodox economists about the originality and validity of MMT. Most of this debate has been about theoretical issues: the validity of MMT's theory of the origins of money; whether money or credit should be the fundamental category; the transmission mechanism of monetary policy and so forth. These theoretical debates are valuable and even necessary. They are the stuff of normal academic exchange, or at least, they should be. But missing from most of this debate has been the empirical validity and policy applicability of MMT ideas. This is surprising since MMT has advocated particular macroeconomic policies.[8]

---

[7] See the references in footnote 1 above.

[8] A lot of the advocacy has been for employer of last resort policies and there has been more of an institutional and empirical discussion of this issue in the literature. My focus, however,

While the economists' debate thus far has shed some important light on theoretical and doctrinal issues, there has been virtually no discussion of the empirical, historical, and institutional validity and limits of the MMT approach to macroeconomic policy. While theoretical and doctrinal discussion can be very useful, empirical assessment is especially important when theories are possibly on the verge of moving from the academic stage to the policy ones.

My book therefore focuses on questions about the validity and policy relevance of MMT's macroeconomic policy proposals. As my title indicates—*What's Wrong with MMT: A Policy Critique*—in the end, I find some significant failings in MMTs macroeconomic policies. The rest of this book describes these limitations and problems.

In particular, in the rest of the book, I focus on the monetary and fiscal policy recommendations promulgated by MMT advocates.[9] There are obvious questions about the viability of MMT macro-policies: what would be their impacts on inflation, exchange rate instability, interest rates, financial instability, investment and economic growth? What, ultimately, are the limits and constraints on MMT macro-policy?

Wray and other MMT analysts have recognized some of these issues, and have discussed them in various writings, including Wray's 2012 "Primer."[10] But, in my view, MMT advocates have not sufficiently addressed the institutional, empirical, and policy realities of the modern international financial system and their implications for the limitations on MMT policy.[11] My conclusion is that, when one takes into account the substantial empirical

---

is on the fiscal and monetary policies advocated by MMT. Here there has been almost no empirical and institutional discussion.

[9] I am aware that there is a debate within MMT circles about whether MMT should exclusively focus on "descriptive" issues or should also address "normative" ones (Wray 2012). Galbraith (2019) defends MMT, for example, by arguing that it is mostly a descriptive theory, not a policy one. My book focuses on the validity of key policy and political messages of MMT so I focus on the normative claims. For a summary of these, see Wray (2012, chap. 6). In this book I will not address various doctrinal or theoretical issues concerning the nature of "sovereign money," the role of money vs. credit, and so forth, except insofar as these address the specific focus of the book.

[10] See, for example, Wray, pp. 112 and 189, and my discussion below.

[11] There are exceptions. MMT analysts have carefully studied some of the institutional limitations in the Euro Zone (see, for example, Wray 2012, Sections 5.6–5.9), and their proposal for Employer of Last Resort (ELR), has paid close attention to institutional details (see Tcherneva 2018).

and institutional literature that has studied these issues, the applicability of MMT policy proposals, is, at best, extremely limited.

I can summarize my argument briefly here. In Chapter 2, I provide the brief basics on the MMT approach to monetary and fiscal policy as a background for the rest of the book. I then discuss the determinants of key variables that are important to our discussion of fiscal and monetary policy, including the determinants of inflation and hyperinflation, the impacts of government deficits, and the impacts of monetary policy.

In Chapter 3, I explain why the global applicability of MMT is very limited. Even though MMT advocates claim that its macroeconomic framework applies to all countries with "sovereign currencies," there is significant evidence that it does not apply to the vast majority of such countries in the developing world that are integrated into modern global financial markets. As is well-known, in the modern world, these countries are subject to the vagaries of international capital flows, sometimes called "sudden stops." The problem is that, in light of these flows, these countries have limited fiscal and monetary policy space, surely insufficient to conduct MMT prescribed monetary and fiscal policies for full employment. Wray argues that flexible exchange rates would provide sufficient policy space for these countries to undertake MMT macro-policies. Occasionally he briefly mentions capital controls but these are not seriously discussed as a complementary policy.[12] But, I argue that a careful survey of the empirical evidence casts grave doubts on the effectiveness of flexible rates for giving policy autonomy or insulating these countries from the vagaries of global financial flows. This problem is worse for countries that cannot borrow in their own currencies, but also applies to small open countries that are able to borrow in their own currencies. The upshot is that the number of countries to whom MMT might apply is quite limited, namely, only countries that issue their own internationally accepted currency.

Chapter 4 explores the limits of exploiting the international role of the dollar in the pursuit of MMT policy. Even for those countries that issue their own international currencies, the sustainability and "exploitability" of the international role is not absolute. The country that has the greatest fiscal and monetary space is the United States, which issues the predominant key currency, the US dollar. Whereas Wray has written that the predominance

---

[12] See Wray's cursory mentions on pp. 139, 211, 216. William Mitchell is the main MMT economist who discusses capital controls as a way of protecting developing country macroeconomic autonomy. I discuss Mitchell's contributions later.

of the dollar is not something we will need to worry about in our lifetime, historical and empirical evidence suggests that even considerable forces for persistence of key currency positions can weaken over time, perhaps even rapidly and dramatically.[13] This is especially true when there are competing currencies with both a "will" and a "way" to achieve key currency status. China (and to a lesser extent, the Eurozone) are competitors in this sense. There is significant evidence of a move to a multicurrency system in which dollar holders can more easily switch out of the dollar if significant, perceived problems arise, such as high exchange rate instability, or excessive inflation. In such a world, the ability of the US government to exploit the dollar's "exorbitant privilege" to sustain very large debt levels or sustained low interest rates will have limits. To be sure, these limits are uncertain, but history suggests that the US cannot completely ignore them, even in "our" lifetime.

But even if the dollar's role continues indefinitely to create space to implement MMT macro-policies, that doesn't mean that the US should actually do so. Chapter 5 argues that The MMT proposed policy amounts to an "America First" macroeconomic policy. While it is traditional for the US (and other countries) to ignore the impacts of their macroeconomic policies on the rest of the world, presumably a progressive approach to policy would adopt a more internationalist perspective. There is significant evidence that there are substantial spillover effects of US monetary policy on emerging market and developing countries that are transmitted largely through the dollar's predominant international role. These spillover effects can be highly destabilizing if the Federal Reserve pursues excessively loose or tight monetary policy without any consideration of their impacts on developing countries. For example, as Jane D'Arista (2019) shows, the low interest rates of the Greenspan era helped to generate dangerous levels of dollar-denominated leverage in emerging markets which contributed to the spread of financial crisis in 2007–2008. A more internationalist, progressive approach to macroeconomic would take these impacts into account. At a minimum, to address these impacts, MMT analysts would have to evaluate institutional arrangements such as capital controls, and financial regulations to mitigate these negative impacts. These receive at most only a cursory mention in their work.

---

[13] See Wray's claim on p. 72 (Wray 2012).

MMT advocates might argue that their proposed low US interest rates would facilitate growth in developing countries by reducing the cost of capital for these countries, so that the spillovers would be good, not bad. But by itself, this claim ignores the highly speculative nature of modern international financial markets. A careful analysis of the impact of low, long-term interest rates shows that in the absence of strong financial regulations domestically and internationally, the impact is likely to be the accumulation of high leverage, asset bubbles and financial instability. Yet MMT theorists talk very little in the context of their proposed macroeconomic policies about the necessary role of financial regulations and capital account regulations in channeling funds productively and limiting financial crises. This lacuna is puzzling in view of MMT theorists' long-standing association with the work of Hyman Minsky. In short, this relative lack of attention to financial instability and financial regulation in the context of their proposed monetary and fiscal policy is a key example of their relative inattention to institutional and empirical constraints on the macroeconomic policies they propose. Chapter 6 explores these issues.

Chapter 7 raises grave concerns about the political implications of the MMT macro-policy approach. As I mentioned earlier, much of MMT's policy appeal stems from the strong perception that MMT implies that progressives with programmatic plans do not need to say or worry about the costs of these programs or how they are going to be "paid for." But even within the framework of MMT itself, this claim of a free lunch is incorrect. Recall that MMT theorists recognize that at or around full employment, further economic expansion could lead to an increase in inflation and if this fiscal and monetary expansion were pushed too far, inflation could accelerate. In this world, at full employment, MMT theorists argue that the government would have to raise taxes or cut private or other public spending in order to make room for new fiscal initiatives. This is no free lunch. Yet, MMT advocates do not emphasize this point in a systematic way to their would-be followers. I believe this presents a serious danger for progressive policy.[14]

Chapter 8 concludes by briefly describing what a more viable progressive approach to monetary and fiscal policy would look like in our current time.

---

[14] A recent working paper by Nersisyan and Wray (2019) acknowledge that large programs like "A Green New Deal" are likely to have to be "paid for," though they do not use that terminology.

References

Blanchard, Olivier. 2019. "Public Debt and Low Interest Rates." AEA Presidential Address.

Blanchard, Olivier, and Lawrence Summers. 2017. *Rethinking Stabilization Policy: Evolution or Revolution?* (No. w24179). Cambridge, MA: National Bureau of Economic Research.

Blyth, Mark. 2013. *Austerity: The History of a Dangerous Idea*. Oxford and New York: Oxford University Press.

Carter, Zach. 2018. "Stephanie Has the Biggest Idea in Washington." Huffpost. Accessed June 15, 2019.

Crotty, James. 2019. *Keynes Against Capitalism: His Economic Case for Liberal Socialism*, 1st ed. Series: Economics as Social Theory. New York: Routledge.

D'Arista, Jane. 2019. *All Fall Down: Debt, Deregulation and Financial Crises*. Northampton: E. Elgar Press.

Dymski, Gary, Gerald A. Epstein, and Robert Pollin (eds.). 1993. *Transforming the U.S. Financial System: Equity and Efficiency for the 21st Century*. Armonk, NY: M.E. Sharpe.

Englander, Steve. 2019. "Modern Monetary Theory for Conservatives." FX Alert, Standard Charter, April 15.

Epstein, Gerald, and Erinc Yeldan, eds. 2009. *Beyond Inflation Targeting: Monetary Policy for Employment Generation and Poverty Reduction*. Northampton, MA: Edward Elgar Press.

Furman, Jason. 2016. "The New View of Fiscal Policy and Its Application". Speech, New York City.

Galbraith, James K. 2012. *Inequality and Instability: A Study of the World Economy Just Before the Great Crisis*, 1st ed. New York, NY: Oxford University Press.

Galbraith, James. 2019. "Modern Monetary Realism." Project Syndicate, March 15.

Guida, Victoria. 2019. "Ocasio-Cortez Boosts Progressive Theory That Deficits Aren't So Scary." Politico, February 6.

Henwood, Doug. 2019. "Modern Monetary Theory Isn't Helping." *Jacobin Magazine*, Issue 2, February.

Herndon, Thomas, Michael Ash, and Robert Pollin. 2014. "Does High Public Debt Consistently Stifle Economic Growth? A Critique of Reinhart and Rogoff." *Cambridge Journal of Economics* 38 (2): 257–279.

Holland, Ben, and Matthew Boesler. 2019. "MMT Has Been Around for Decades. Here's Why It Just Caught Fire." Bloomberg, March 11.

Kelton, Stephanie. 2019. "The Wealthy Are Victims of Their Own Propaganda." Bloomberg. Accessed June 15, 2019.

Lavoie, Marc. 2013. "The Monetary and Fiscal Nexus of Neo-Chartalism: A Friendly Critique." *Journal of Economic Issues* 47 (1), 1–32.

Lerner, Abba. 1943. "Functional Finance and the Federal Debt." *Social Research* 10, 38–51.

McCormick, Liz. 2019. "Jerome Powell Says the Concept of MMT Is 'Just Wrong'." Bloomberg, February 26.

Mehrling, Perry. 2000. "Modern Money: Fiat or Credit?" *Journal of Post Keynesian Economics* 22 (3): 397–406.

Nersisyan, Yeva, and L. Randall Wray. 2019. "How to Pay for the Green New Deal." *SSRN Scholarly Paper ID3398983*. Rochester, NY: Social Science Research Network. https://papers.ssrn.com/abstract=3398983.

Newmeyer, Tory. 2019. "The Finance 202: Larry Kudlow Dismisses Deficit Concerns as GOP Abandons Fiscal Toughness." *The Washington Post*, June 14.

Palley, Thomas I. 2015a. "The Critics of Modern Money Theory (MMT) Are Right." *Review of Political Economy* 27 (1): 45–61.

Palley, Thomas I. 2015b. "Money, Fiscal Policy, and Interest Rates: A Critique of Modern Monetary Theory." *Review of Political Economy* 27 (1): 1–23.

Palley, Thomas I. 2019a. "What's Wrong with Modern Money Theory (MMT): A Critical Primer." Forum For Macroeconomics and Macroeconomic Policies No. 44, March.

Palley, Thomas I. 2019b. "Macroeconomics vs. Modern Money Theory: Some Unpleasant Keynesian Arithmetic." Post Keynesian Economics Society, Working Paper No. 1910, April.

Pollin, Robert. 2003. *Contours of Descent: US Economic Fractures and the Landscape of Global Austerity*. London: Verso Press.

Reinhart, Carmen M., and Kenneth S. Rogoff. 2010. "Growth in a Time of Debt." *American Economic Review* 100 (2): 573–578.

Robinson, Joan. 1974. "What Has Become of the Keynesian Revolution?" *Challenge* 16 (6): 6–11.

Rogoff, Kenneth. 2019. "Modern Monetary Nonsense." Project Syndicate, March 4.

Taylor, L. 2008. "A Foxy Hedgehog: Wynne Godley and Macroeconomic Modelling." *Cambridge Journal of Economics* 32 (4): 639–663.

Tcherneva, Pavlina R. 2018. "The Job Guarantee: Design, Jobs, and Implementation." *SSRN Electronic Journal*.

Tymoigne, Eric. 2009. *Central Banking, Asset Prices and Financial Fragility*. New York: Routledge.

Vernengo, Matías. 2016. Curried Keynesianism Meets the Master: Lauchlin Currie's Memorandum on The General Theory for the Federal Reserve Board. *Review of Keynesian Economics* 4 (1): 56–60.

Waldman, Paul. 2019. "The Man Who Liberated the Republican Party; How Arthur Laffer Taught the GOP to Govern Without Constraint." *The American Prospect*, June 10.

Wray, L. Randall. 2012. *Modern Money Theory: A Primer on Macroeconomics for Sovereign Monetary Systems*. London: Palgrave Macmillan.

CHAPTER 2

MMT Basics and the Sustainability of Money Financed Deficits

Abstract MMT is a type of post-Keynesian economics that has two distinctive components: (1) chartalism, a type of state money theory; and (2) functional finance, due to Abba Lerner, the idea that the role of taxes is not to finance spending but rather to inject or drain spending in order to maintain full employment without inflation. These ideas lead MMT advocates to claim that governments that issue sovereign money do not need to pay for spending, imply that the level of government debt has no negative consequences for such countries because such countries "cannot go bankrupt," and suggest that the central banks' role is to finance government spending, preferably at permanently low interest rates. This chapter investigates the general validity of these propositions.

Keywords Chartalism · Sovereign money · Debt monetization

In theoretical and policy debates, you can often hear MMT advocates make claims like the following[1]:

It is Impossible for the US To Default. (John T. Harvey 2012)

---

[1] I am using here Lavoie (2013, 10) for a convenient compilation of many of these and then added a few of my own.

© The Author(s) 2019
G. A. Epstein, *What's Wrong with Modern Money Theory?*,
https://doi.org/10.1007/978-3-030-26504-5_2

A sovereign government can always make payments as they come due by crediting bank accounts — something recognized by Chairman Ben Bernanke when he said the Fed spends by marking up the size of the reserve accounts of banks. (*L. Randall Wray*, as quoted in Harvey 2012)

Taxes do not finance spending. (Forstater and Mosler 2005, 538)

The Treasury does not "need" to borrow in order to deficit-spend. (Wray 1998, 117)

Neither taxes nor bonds really finance government spending on any reasonable definition of the term finance. (Bell and Wray 2002, 269)

…Government spends simply by crediting a private sector bank account at the central bank. Operationally, this process is independent of any prior revenue, including taxing and borrowing. (Mitchell and Muysken 2008)

… we can pay for a Green New Deal and that the obsession with finding a dollar of new "revenue" to offset every new dollar of spending is the wrong way to approach the federal budgeting process. My views belong to the macroeconomic school of thought known as Modern Monetary Theory — MMT, for short. … (explains) that when Congress approves a budget, the Treasury Department instructs the Federal Reserve to credit a seller's bank account. (Kelton 2019)

The 'Tax the Rich' call bestows unwarranted importance on them. (Bill Mitchell, February 21, 2019)

Deficit spending…would cause the Fed Funds rate to fall. (Mosler 2009, 12)

Many people find these statements empowering; others intriguing; and others find at least some of them simply stupefying.

What do MMT advocates mean by statements like these? What is the basis for them? How valid are they?

First, let's start with the basics.

2.1 What Is Modern Money Theory?

Modern Money Theory (MMT) is a brand of Post-Keynesian economic theory that, like other varieties of post-Keynesian thought, has received inspiration from John Maynard Keynes (of course), Joan Robinson, Hyman Minsky, and others.[2] Along with most other Post-Keynesians (and Keynes and Minsky), MMT advocates emphasize the key role of aggregate demand in determining output and employment in both the short and long run, the central role of money and finance in the workings of the economy, and the importance of endogenous money.[3] These tenets contrast starkly with the mainstream view that supply-side factors alone determine employment in the long run, and, that long-run unemployment itself cannot exist; that money is a "veil" hiding the workings of the "real" economy while not impacting its long-run trajectory (apart from the level of prices and, perhaps, inflation); and that the central bank controls key components of the money supply, effectively making the money supply "exogenous" (see Taylor 2011 and Crotty 2019, for excellent statements of these and other key differences).

What makes MMT doctrinally distinctive, though, is its key emphasis on two ideas that are not typically present in other post-Keynesian theory: (1) "Chartalism" and MMT's related concept of "sovereign money" and (2) "Functional Finance," developed by economist Abba Lerner (1943) (see Wray 2012 for a standard presentation, and Lavoie 2013 for an excellent summary and discussion). For MMT, Chartalism and sovereign money are used to explain why (some) countries do not need to worry about running budget deficits since "sovereign money" countries "can never go bankrupt" and functional finance explains that the role of taxes is not to "pay for government expenditures"—which can rather simply be paid for by printing sovereign money—but rather is to drain or create aggregate demand to maintain full employment without inflation, in a "Keynesian" manipulation of aggregate demand. While some other post-Keynesians might subscribe to the ideas of functional finance, the combination of "sovereign money" and "functional finance" is unique to MMT. In light of this combination of ideas, Lavoie (2013) and others refer to MMTers as being "Neo-Chartalists." Taking both of their distinctive tenets into consideration, one could call them "functional financiers" with a Chartalist twist.

---

[2] Some prominent MMT advocates refer to their theory as "Modern Monetary Theory". Others, including Randall Wray who is, perhaps, the preeminent MMT theorist, calls it "Modern Money Theory". Somewhat arbitrarily, I adopt Wray's usage in this book.

[3] Theories of "endogenous money" hold that central banks do not control the money supply; rather, the banking system creates money in the process of making loans. For classic statements see Kaldor (1982) and Moore (1988).

Chartalism is based on an old idea. Chartalists, old and new, argue that the State determines what can serve as money.[4] Importantly, a common version, subscribed to by MMTers argues that the state enforces this decision by requiring that taxes be paid in this money. The theory is called "chartalism" because what serves as money is defined by the state and the ability of banks to produce money is granted by charters (Lavoie 2013, 3).

2.2 Sovereign Money

The concept of "sovereign money" is central to the macroeconomic arguments of MMT. According to MMT theorists, there are degrees of monetary sovereignty; a country with full sovereignty meets the following conditions: the domestic currency is the unit of account; taxes and government expenditures are paid in this currency; the central bank is unhindered by regulations; the public debt is issued in the domestic currency; and there is a regime of pure floating exchange rates (Wray 2002, 24; Lavoie 2013, 4).

Clearly, very few countries comply with all these requirements.[5] Yet, in practice, MMT analysts often suggest that countries even with lesser degrees of "monetary sovereignty" can nonetheless successfully implement MMT style macroeconomic policies. Much of the rest of this book, and especially Chapters 3, 4 and 5 addresses this issue.

Another distinctive aspect of MMT is their policy focus on the "employer of last resort" (ELR) scheme to maintain full employment (see Tcherneva 2018). This is a particular policy proposal designed to implement a key goal of MMT analysis: to maintain full employment. In fact, many of the arguments that MMT advocates use in support of the claim that "we do not need to discuss how to pay for government programs" are marshaled in defense of public employment guarantee programs.

In this book, my focus is on the general issues of monetary and fiscal policy and government deficits and taxation, so I will not explicitly deal with ELR schemes. My justifications are that there has already been extensive discussion of these programs (see for example, Tcherneva 2018; Sawyer 2003; Seccareccia 2004), and that an adequate discussion of it would take us too far afield from and are not central to the main argument of the book.

---

[4]Some call this a "state theory" of money. A number of important economists, including Keynes, held this view. It is often subscribed to the work of German Economist Georg Friedrich Knapp who in 1905 published a book entitled *The State Theory of Money*.

[5]Lavoie (2013) suggests Canada does.

Apart from the ELR programs, most of the heterodox academic discussion of MMT has focused on theoretical issues such as the historical validity and mechanisms of chartalism, whether tax payments are sufficient to support the state's definition of money, the relative importance of money and credit in MMT analysis, and the mechanisms of payment and clearing in modern monetary systems (see my short summaries below for references). The debate has also centered on the degree of originality of the main claims of MMT as well as the viability of the kind of "fine-tuning" of macroeconomic policy that MMT analysts sometimes seem to propose (see for example, Palley 2013, 2015).

All of these discussions are important in order to properly assess MMT. But what has largely been missing has been an institutional and, especially, empirical evaluation of MMTs main arguments, especially with respect to their main policy proposals for monetary policy, fiscal policy and taxation. This evaluation is particularly important now that MMT has gotten so much attention for its macroeconomic policy proposals. This is the main subject matter of this book.

The criticisms most germane to my focus on monetary and fiscal policy concern (1) institutional specificity (2) the role of credit, especially endogenous credit, in the MMT scheme (3) taxation and (4) how monetary and fiscal policy would work and what its impacts would be.

Still, it is worthwhile briefly going over some of the more theoretical debates that are most relevant to the main subject of this book—monetary and fiscal policy proposals of MMT.

2.3 Critics: Friendly and Not

Some heterodox economists have been quite critical of MMT claims, like many of those quoted at the start of this chapter. Indeed, Post-Keynesian and other heterodox economists have engaged with MMT arguments for more than a decade. Mainstream discussions and critiques have piled up only recently as part of the recent wave of interest in MMT. I will discuss the heterodox critiques first and briefly mention some of the mainstream critiques after that. To reiterate: I will only focus on those issues that have relevance for the issues I focus on here.

2.4 Monetary and Fiscal Policy Coordination and Institutional Specificity

Many of the perhaps surprising statements listed at the start of this chapter derive from MMTs concept of sovereign money and the relationship that they assume exists between the central bank and the Treasury of a country with a sovereign country. Essentially, they assume that central banks like the Federal Reserve automatically "monetize" government spending. They show this with a flurry of T-accounts; but, as Lavoie argues, for most institutional environments, this "consolidation" of the central bank and the treasury do not exist. For example, the Federal Reserve is prohibited by law from directly buying more than a certain amount of government debt. Instead, they must buy US treasury debt in the secondary market. Hence some of the statements presented at the start that say that the Federal Reserve automatically finances the government's spending is not true. There might be some indirect processes by which this occurs, but these are not always true, and in fact depend on complex political power relations between the Federal Reserve, the President, Congress and private actors—capitalists in general and especially, financiers (Wall Street in the case of the Fed).

Focusing on this point, Lavoie (2013), a self-described "friendly" critic of MMT argues that while MMT theorists are correct about some aspects of their theory, many other claims are based on an assumed institutional structure that in fact does not exist in most countries: a consolidated functioning (balance sheet) between the central bank and the Treasury, a consolidation that does not exist in most countries. Here is an important institutional constraint, pointed out by Lavoie, that shows the importance of institutional specificity and possibly undermines some of the key MMT claims. In the US, specifically, monetary financing of deficits does not happen automatically. The Federal Reserve has to choose to monetize the debt by doing open market operations, and this choice is as much a political one as an economic one. In practice, the Fed has done this occasionally, but rather sparingly.

Wray and other MMT theorists suggest this distinction between the Federal Reserve and the Treasury is just a "veil." They claim that various processes of treasury payment and funds clearing, essentially mean that the Federal Reserve accommodates (effectively monetizes) the Treasury payments. Indeed, this view of Federal Reserve accommodation is a tenet of much post-Keynesian writing on "endogenous money" (see Pollin 1991 for a discussion, critique, and empirical evidence). While it is true that the Treasury and Federal Reserve engage in short-term interactions that tend to engender "debt monetization" in the very short term, the issue here, is the connection in the medium and long term. The debate about the budget deficit and monetary policy is not about short-term monetary accommodation: it is about what the central bank chooses to do about medium-term accommodation versus leaning against the wind. Does it try to keep interest rates low in the medium to long term to facilitate the financing of budget deficits, or does it lean against the wind and raise interest rates. The recent fighting between Donald Trump and the Fed shows that this is a real political issue. It is not obvious, without further political economy analysis, whether Trump or the Fed will win, if they in fact disagree.

To understand this complicated and important relationship requires having an analysis of the political economy of the Federal Reserve in particular and central banks in general (for an extensive discussion of these issues, see Epstein 2019).

In Epstein (2019), I analyze the sources of central bank political power. A key source in the US and many other countries is the political connections between bankers and the central bank. This relationship undergirds the so-called "independence" of central banks and is key in helping to determine the conditions under which central banks accommodate the Treasury or choose not to accommodate. It is no automatic process that can be explained by a flurry of T-accounts. A political economy analysis is required (see also Ferguson [1995]): political backlash from bankers and their allies is what has established and sustained "independent" central banks and austerity policy in the first place.[6] Institutions and power do matter.

2.5 The Central Role of Credit and the Minsky Mystery

As second important critique from Post-Keynesian economists concerns MMT's focus on money, rather than credit as the central macroeconomic financial variable. Again, this comes down to an institutional understanding

---

[6] I agree with those who argue that these central banks are not truly "independent". They are embedded in a complex political economy and power struggle that does not reduce to— they will do whatever the fiscal authorities want—or to they will be completely independent of the government. See Epstein (2019) for a lengthy discussion of these issues.

that matters. Mehrling (2000) has noted that MMT emphasizes money but underplays the role of credit in these discussions. He says that in the modern world, money is a type of credit instrument (see also Taylor 2019). The role of credit is critical for our understanding of some of the main limitations of MMT. This issue of credit in the modern financial economy goes way beyond this point, however. Focusing more on credit allows us to have a window into multiple issues of financial instability, speculation and crisis connected with credit conditions. Kindleberger (1978) noted multiple examples of low interest rates and loose credit conditions leading to excessive lending, asset bubbles and crisis. Since Kindleberger's book came out, many economists have studied the connection between interest rates, credit conditions and financial instability and crisis (see for example, D'Arista 2019). The implications of these findings are not necessarily that low interest rates are always a bad thing; but the thrust of the discussion implies that other institutional policies such as prudential regulations, credit allocation techniques, capital controls, speculation taxes and the like may be needed to accompany low interest rates for them to be effective without leading to financial speculation and crisis (see for example the chapters in Wolfson and Epstein 2013). As I discuss in Chapters 3–6, credit relations and credit cycles have an enormous impact on the viability and sustainability of both monetary and fiscal policy in the US, and elsewhere. It also has a major implication for our understanding of financial regulations necessary to maintain full employment and socially desirable credit allocation. As I discuss in Chapter 6, looking at the domestic and global financial system through a credit rather than through a money lens, means that financial regulations only over banks will not be sufficient to maintain financial stability. Broader financial regulations over the creators of credit and credit like financial instruments, including hedge funds and financial traders, is necessary to maintain full employment and financial stability. The key role of credit will help explain some of the limitations on low long-term interest rates as proposed by MMT analysts, in the absence of financial regulations that will impact the broader financial system.

2.6 MMT's Proposals for Monetary and Fiscal Policy

The key MMT macroeconomic policy proposal is that government spending should target full employment, and that the central bank should keep interest rates low by monetizing the debt.[7] Moreover, the government should not worry about "financing the budget" through taxes or cuts in other spending. This is functional finance with an MMT twist. MMT advocates argue that at full employment, the fiscal authorities should raise taxes or cut spending to drain demand from the economy to maintain full employment without inflation (Wray 2012; Palley 2013, 2015; Tymoigne and Wray 2015). In this rendering, then, macroeconomic policy should be guided by fiscal spending to achieve full employment, and the policy should be subject to an inflation constraint managed by fiscal policy tools. Monetary policy, in turn, should focus on keeping the interest rate low. Palley has addressed the problems of using fiscal policy to fine-tune the economy to reach full employment without excessive inflation (Palley 2013, 2015). These are familiar from the old debates about fine-tuning vs. rules and emphasize uncertain lags, uncertain shocks to the economy, and poor understanding of key parameters such as multipliers associated with different policies and the shape and position of the Philips Curve. In addition, there are many related problems associated with this idea of fine-tuning fiscal policy at the point of full employment: how exactly do we define full employment? What about underemployment? What about variations in labor force participation rates over the cycle? There are additional problems. What happens when the economy crosses the threshold between the unemployment/low taxes world and to the full employment/higher taxes world: Let's say we do know where to set the full employment threshold. We are now introducing a massive shock into the economy when we cross into full employment. That is, just before full employment taxes are very low. After we cross the threshold, all of a sudden, the government is collecting a significant amount of taxes. How do we avoid a significant destabilization?[8]

---

[7]In the US, the Fed would monetize the debt by buying government securities on the open market because the Fed is prohibited by law from lending directly to the Treasury. See Fiebiger (2012).

[8]Thanks to Robert Pollin for pointing out these complications.

2.7 What Are the Impacts of MMT Macroeconomic Policies? What Are the Limits and Constraints on Them?

What are the macroeconomic impacts of running large central bank financed budget deficits? This is where much of the controversy with mainstream economists lies, and with some heterodox economists. It is also a key focus of this book. MMT has recently come under attack by prominent mainstream economists and policymakers, including Kenneth Rogoff, former chief economist at the IMF, Lawrence Summers, former Secretary of the Treasury and Jerome Powell, current chair of the Federal Reserve. These economists and officials have accused MMT proponents and the progressive politicians who have spoken favorably about them, of endangering fundamental macroeconomic stability, and even possibly causing "hyperinflation" and an "exchange rate collapse." For the case of the US, these most dire scenarios are misplaced, and MMT analysts and other heterodox economists are correct to counter them.

2.8 Hyperinflation

MMT advocates correctly argue that debt monetization and increases in the supply of money are not, by themselves, typically a cause of hyperinflation. They correctly claim that most hyperinflations are due to profound structural disruptions in economies, such as famines or wars or gross mismanagement on the supply side of the economy, not the demand side. Excessive foreign debt can play a role in some cases to be sure. The hyperinflation in Germany in the 1920s, for example, was due to the supply shortages generated by the war combined with reparation demands from the Treaty of Versailles. As Kindleberger shows, it was exacerbated by a depreciating exchange rate due to financial speculation (Kindelberger 1993, chap. 17). There is virtually no evidence that increases in the money supply, or debt monetization, in the context of a well-functioning supply side of the economy (and proper management of demand, see below), is likely to lead to hyperinflation. In short, there is a massive literature on the causes of hyperinflations in different historical episodes and as Wray and many others have argued, these causes are extremely diverse and cannot be reduced to simplistic explanations of excessive debt accumulation or excessive monetary easing.

2.9 The Unsustainability of High Debt Levels

The MMT argument that the sustainability of public debt levels should not be a concern at any level is more questionable. As one of the quotes above indicates, sometimes they mean by this simply that, in sovereign currency countries, countries cannot be forced to default because they can always just print money. But this is of little macroeconomic importance. For that, we are concerned about the macroeconomic impacts of very high and growing levels of public debt. Sometimes, MMT theorists do discuss the term "sustainability" in its more common (and important) meaning in terms of the macroeconomic impacts of high levels of debt (Wray 2012, 66–75). In fact, the evidence on this point for developed countries is quite murky and uncertain (developing countries are a different matter and treated in the next chapter). I already mentioned the devastating empirical critique by Herndon et al. (2014) of the iconic study by Reinhart and Rogoff (2010) which purported to show that economic growth falls off a cliff after a threshold level of public debt to GDP of around 90%. HAP showed that this threshold does not exist. Follow up work by Ash et al. (2018) delve further into causality issues to show that in the case of advanced capitalist countries, there is little to no evidence that higher debt levels cause reductions in economic growth, and within the range of debt levels that characterize these countries, there is no sign of a threshold in terms of causality. Still, of course, these results do not speak to debt levels higher than that experienced in their data set. Thus, these results are not definitive for all levels that might be reached if an MMT policy were implemented. This remains an area of uncertainty and potential concern. That being said, another factor might allay this concern in the current period. Evidence on current financing costs on public debt relative to growth rates also should reduce concerns about debt sustainability in the immediate period. A commonly understood relationship indicates that debt "sustainability," defined as a bounded public debt to GDP ratio, hinges importantly on the rate of growth of GDP relative to the interest rate on debt. Pollin showed several years ago that financing costs on US debt were going down because of the low existing interest rates generated by central banks and stemming from the sluggish world economic growth (Pollin 2010). A recent study by an IMF economist joins a number of recent papers showing that for advanced capitalist countries in the last five decades or so, interest rates on government debt are often below the growth rate of the economy (Barrett 2018, and the references therein). With a negative "interest rate minus growth rate" level, any ratio of debt to GDP is sustainable, as long as annual deficits do not grow at too high a rate. Note that this finding does not mean that increases in the level of budget deficits can be unbounded: on the contrary, they are constrained by the size and stability of the gap between interest rates and growth rates.[9] In addition, while Barrett shows that this factor (growth rate—interest rate) has on average been negative for long periods of time, it does fluctuate and in some periods for some countries, it jumps up to positive territory, where high debt levels can begin to grow from debt service at a rate higher than GDP driving the ratio of debt to GDP to higher and higher levels. Barrett's empirical analysis suggests that there is some uncertainty as to whether the relationship between interest rates and growth rates is steady enough to warrant a highly aggressive public debt growth strategy. Moreover, there is of course uncertainty about future growth rates relative to interest rates. Still, Barrett's empirical results and those of others suggest that the constraints on advanced countries' public debt accumulation in an era of low interest rates are much looser than the austerity hawks have suggested (see also Furman and Summers 2019).

MMT analysts, such as Randall Wray, have argued that for sovereign money countries, this ratio can always be made negative because the central bank controls the interest rate (Wray 2012, 71–75.) But there are many interest rates, and even central banks with a lot of policy space like the Federal Reserve can only easily control only its policy rate which might not be the rate most relevant for financing government debt.

Moreover, the key rate that mostly matters for investment and other critical variables are inflation adjusted interest rates and even powerful central banks like the Fed do not have complete control of that, especially if they have committed to permanent low interest rates.

Mason and Jayadev (2018) have addressed this question of debt financing vs. monetary financing of budget deficits in the context of MMT. They argue that the issue of the validity of the MMT argument can be analyzed in terms of the familiar assignment problem in macroeconomic policy analysis, built on the work of Tinbergen and Mundell. They claim that the debate over MMT can be framed in terms of two goals for macro policy—full employment and stable public debt to GDP ratio—and two instruments—fiscal policy and interest rates (monetary policy). The assignment problem asks if you assign one instrument to each target, what should

---

[9] The growth rate of the budget deficit must also not keep going up indefinitely.

the assignment be? Mason and Jayadev show that in a closed economy context, it doesn't matter when debt levels are low, but, paradoxically, at high debt levels, fiscal policy should be assigned to maintaining full employment and monetary policy should be assigned to sustaining the debt levels by keeping interest rates low—what they call "the MMT (or functional finance) solution." As we have just seen, the economics behind this argument is that at high debt levels, it is critical to keep interest rates low so that their growth rate from servicing costs does not get out of hand.[10] Still, the Mason and Jayadev discussion as a defense of MMT leaves out some crucial issues. First, MMT analysts have not accepted the need to maintain a target federal debt to GDP level. Their argument is that sovereign money can "finance" any debt level. Second, the Mason and Jayadev analysis ignores important financial market issues and open economy considerations. In particular, in the domestic arena they do not consider the impact of low interest rates on private debt accumulation and the possibility of financial speculation and asset bubbles; and, in terms of open economy issues, they do not consider the spillover impacts from the US to the rest of the world. They also do not consider whether their model applies to a country that does not issue an international currency, so in their model, there are no exchange rate, or international financial speculation constraints. Thus, their interpretation is subject to the same limitations that plague MMT macroeconomic analysis in general.

Even though MMT theorists deny that rapidly growing public deficit and debt levels can be a serious problem for sovereign money countries, they nonetheless do recognize some relevant constraints on fiscal policy. Wray (2012) discussed possible limits and constraints on policy this way: He argues that: "Just because government can spend doesn't mean that government ought to spend" (Wray 2012, 187) and proceeds to discuss possible legitimate limits or constraints on government spending: (1) too much spending can cause inflation (2) too much spending can pressure the exchange rate (3) too much spending by government might leave too few resources for private interests (4) government should not do everything—impacts on incentives could be perverse (5) budgeting provides a lever to manage and evaluate government projects (Wray 2012, 188.) These are reasonable points and suggest a research agenda of careful theoretical and,

---

[10] As Palley notes, their discussion follows on a large literature by Keynesian economists of the government budget constraint and the impacts of debt vs. monetary financing on the growth and stability of the economy (see for example, Blinder and Solow 1973).

more importantly, empirical analysis of these possible constraints in different contexts. But to my knowledge, MMT advocates have not implemented such a research agenda for the United States or any other country.

2.10 Functional Finance and Fine-Tuning Macroeconomic Policy

Palley has addressed the problems of using fiscal policy to fine-tune the economy to reach full employment without excessive inflation (Palley 2013, 2015) There are many related problems associated with this idea of fine-tuning fiscal policy at the point of full employment: how exactly do we define full employment? What about underemployment? What about variations in labor force participation rates over the cycle?

Wray (2012) explores these constraints casually. I have already mentioned the argument (which is common to MMT's interpretation of "functional finance") that when the economy reaches full employment, the government should use fiscal policy to "drain" demand from the economy to avoid excessive (and possibly accelerating) inflation. I will discuss this at some length, especially in Chapter 7. Wray's second potential constraint "too much spending can pressure the exchange rate" is importantly related to the issues addressed in this paper. This becomes especially important for understanding the possible constraints to MMT type policy undertaken by developing countries as I discuss in the next few chapters. The main implications of these contributions are as follows: Under current conditions of low interest rate and global financial markets, there is very good evidence that the austerity focused mainstream economists of both Republican and Democratic ilk in the US and similar stripes in Europe, have greatly exaggerated the dangers of budget deficits and growing debt for advanced economies. This point aligns with some of the claims of MMT, and especially, the functional finance perspective. At the same time, the reluctance, of MMT economists to take seriously institutional constraints on their analysis and policy raises serious questions about the validity of their arguments in the context of real-world environments: the ability to fine-tune fiscal policy to implement MMT policy; the institutional configuration of central banks in relation to fiscal authorities; and the key role of credit and broad financial institutions and markets in the dynamics of the modern national and global economy, are all important elements demanding much more empirical and institutional analysis and raise serious concerns about the validity of MMT policy ideas. Even if these concerns were resolved, there are still further institutional issues and constraints that render MMT type policy quite particular and applicable, if anywhere to a small slice of humanity: mainly those living in countries with international currencies and especially the US. As the next chapter shows, there is a significant amount of empirical research demonstrating that fiscal and monetary policy space is highly constrained in developing countries, even those that have "sovereign currencies." It also shows that "flexible exchange rates" alone are no panacea that will set these countries free, as some advocates of MMT have claimed.

REFERENCES

Ash, Michael, Deepankar Basu, and Arindrajit Dube. 2018. "Public Debt and Growth: An Assessment of Key Findings on Causality and Thresholds." UMass Economics Department Working Paper.

Barrett, Philip. 2018. *Interest-Growth Differentials and Debt Limits in Advanced Economies*. Washington, DC: International Monetary Fund. http://public.eblib.com/choice/publicfullrecord.aspx?p=5377991.

Bell, Stephanie, and L. Randall Wray. 2002. "Fiscal Effects on Reserves and the Independence of the Fed." *Journal of Post Keynesian Economics* 25 (2): 263–271.

Blinder, Alan, and Robert Solow. 1973. "Does Fiscal Policy Matter." *Journal of Public Economics* 2 (4): 319–337.

Crotty, James R. 2019. *Keynes Against Capitalism: His Economic Case for Liberal Socialism*. New York: Routledge.

D'Arista, Jane. 2019. *All Fall Down*. Northampton, MA: Edward Elgar Press.

Epstein, Gerald. 2019. *The Political Economy of Central Banking: Contested Control and the Power of Finance*. Northampton, MA: Edward Elgar Press.

Ferguson, Thomas. 1995. "*Golden Rule: The Investment Theory of Party Competition and the Logic of Money-Driven Political Systems*." Chicago: University of Chicago Press.

Fiebiger, Brett, Scott Fullwiler, Stephanie Kelton, and L. Randall Wray. 2012. *Modern Monetary Theory: A Debate* Working Papers wp279, Political Economy Research Institute, University of Massachusetts at Amherst.

Furman, Jason, and Lawrence Summers. 2019. "Who's Afraid of Budget Deficits." *Foreign Affairs*, January.

Forstater, Mathew, and Warren Mosler. 2005. "The Natural Rate of Interest Is Zero." *Journal of Economic Issues* 39 (2): 535–542.

Harvey, John T. 2012. "It Is Impossible for the US to Default." October 9, 2012. https://www.forbes.com/sites/johntharvey/2012/09/10/impossible-to-default/#14699bc71180.

Herndon, Thomas, Michael Ash, and Robert Pollin. 2014. "Does High Public Debt Consistently Stifle Economic Growth? A Critique of Reinhart and Rogoff." *Cambridge Journal of Economics* 38 (2): 257–279.
Kaldor, Nicholas. 1982. *The Scourge of Monetarism*. Oxford: Oxford University Press.
Kelton, Stephanie. 2019. "The Wealthy Are Victims of Their Own Propaganda." *Bloomberg*. Accessed June 15, 2019.
Kindleberger, Charles P. 1978 and later editions. *Manias, Panics and Crashes*. New York: Basic Books.
Kindleberger, Charles P. 1993. *A Financial History of Western Europe*. 2nd Edition. New York: Oxford University Press.
Lavoie, Marc. 2013. "The Monetary and Fiscal Nexus of Neo-Chartalism: A Friendly Critique." *Journal of Economic Issues* 47 (1): 1–32.
Lerner, Abba. 1943. "Functional Finance and the Federal Debt." *Social Research* 10: 38–51.
Mason, J. W., and Arjun Jayadev. 2018. "A Comparison of Monetary and Fiscal Policy Interaction Under 'Sound' and 'Functional' Finance Regimes." *Metroeconomica* 69 (2): 488–508.
Mehrling, Perry. 2000. "Modern Money: Fiat or Credit?" *Journal of Post Keynesian Economics* 22 (3): 397–406.
Mitchell, William, and J. Muysken. 2008. *Full Employment Abandoned: Shifting Sands and Policy Failures*. Cheltenham, UK and Northampton, MA: Edward Elgar.
Mosler, Warren. 2009. "Proposals for the Treasury, the Federal Reserve, the FDIC, and the Banking System." Warren Mosler Blog.
Moore, Basil. 1988. *Horizontlists and Verticalists: The Macroeconomics of Credit Money*. Cambridge: Cambridge University Press.
Palley, Thomas I. 2013. "Money, Fiscal Policy, and Interest Rates: A Critique of Modern Monetary Theory."
Palley, Thomas I. 2015. "The Critics of Modern Money Theory (MMT) Are Right." *Review of Political Economy* 27 (1): 45–61.
Pollin, Robert. 1991. "Two Theories of Money Supply Endogeneity: Some Empirical Evidence." *Journal of Post Keynesian Economics* 13 (3): 366–396.
Pollin, Robert. 2010. "Austerity Is Not a Solution: Why the Deficit Hawks Are Wrong." *Challenge Magazine*, November/December.
Reinhart, Carmen M., and Kenneth S. Rogoff. 2010. "Growth in a Time of Debt." *American Economic Review: Papers & Proceedings* 100: 573–578.
Sawyer, Malcolm. 2003. "Employer of Last Resort: Could It Deliver Full Employment and Price Stability?" *Journal of Economic Issues* 37 (4): 881–909.
Seccareccia, Mario. 2004. "What Type of Full Employment? A Critical Evaluation of Government as He Employer of Last Resort Policy Proposal." *Investigacion Economica* 63 (247): 15–43.
Taylor, Lance. 2011. *Maynard's Revenge*. Cambridge: Harvard University Press.

Taylor, Lance. 2019. "Macroeconomic Stimulus à la MMT." INET. https://www.ineteconomics.org/perspectives/blog/macroeconomic-stimulus-%C3%A0-la-mmt.
Tcherneva, Pavlina. 2018. "The Job Guarantee: Design, Jobs, and Implementation." *SSRN Electronic Journal*.
Tymoigne, Eric, and L. Randall Wray. 2015. "Modern Money Theory: A Reply to Palley." *Review of Political Economy* 27 (1), 24–44.
Wolfson, Martin H., and Gerald A. Epstein, eds. 2013. *The Handbook of the Political Economy of Financial Crises*. New York, NY: Oxford University Press.
Wray, L. Randall. 1998. *Understanding Modern Money*. Cheltenham: Edward Elgar, 1998.
Wray, L. Randall. 2002. "State Money." *International Journal of Political Economy* 32 (3): 23–40.
Wray, L. Randall. 2012. *Modern Money Theory: A Primer on Macroeconomics for Sovereign Monetary Systems*. London: Palgrave Macmillan.

CHAPTER 3

Institutional Specificity and the Limited Policy Relevance of Modern Money Theory

Abstract MMTers claim that their perspective applies to all countries that do not borrow extensively in foreign currencies and that have adopted flexible exchange rates. This chapter presents evidence that developing countries borrowing in their own currencies and adopting flexible exchange rates still have significant problems conducting full employment macroeconomic policy. Only those countries that issue major international currencies, particularly the US, has the possible potential to conduct MMT policy. To enhance the ability of developing countries to pursue full employment macro policies, additional tools such as capital controls are likely to be necessary. While some MMT theorists have written about capital controls, their work is not sufficiently detailed and institutionally specific to assess the viability and effectiveness of such policies in practice.

Keywords Hot money flows · Flexible exchange rates · Capital controls

3.1 Introduction

MMT advocates argue that MMT style policy applies to any country with a sovereign currency, though they acknowledge that small open economy countries from the Global South might have less policy space generally than large rich countries (see, for example, Wray 2012, chaps. 3, 5, and 6). Wray argues, furthermore, that the key to MMT policy in smaller or poorer countries with sovereign currencies is to operate a flexible exchange rate (see, for example, Wray 2012, 129 and Chapter 6). Occasionally he briefly mentions capital controls but these are not seriously discussed as a complementary policy.[1] William Mitchell, an Australian economist and avid blogger, does discuss at some length the role of capital controls (e.g., Mitchell 2016). I will return later to a discussion of Mitchell's contributions.

Unfortunately, Wray's claims that flexible exchange rates will enable developing countries to implement MMT style macroeconomic policies do not appear to be backed up by rigorous empirical work. In this chapter, I will try to help fill this gap by referring to systematic empirical studies that have addressed these issues.[2] The empirical work suggests that contrary to MMT claims, many economies with sovereign currencies are forced to stop well short of full employment because of financial speculation and "sudden stops" of capital from international capital markets. This is true in regimes of both fixed and flexible exchange rates. These results strongly suggest that, to the extent that MMT theory applies, it applies only to countries that issue important international currencies. A broader literature, which I will briefly discuss toward the end of this chapter, do address how non-key currency countries can enhance their policy spaces, but this requires a set of institutional innovations such as broader central bank policies, capital management techniques, and other policies.[3] While heterodox economists have studied these institutional constraints and institutional alternatives for decades, as far as I know, MMT theorists, with the exception of William Mitchell, have not, even though such institutional innovations would be necessary to achieve the kind of fiscal space they assume exists for developing countries with sovereign currencies.[4]

---

[1] See Wray's (2012) cursory mentions on pages 139, 211, 216.

[2] Esra Nur Uğurlu prepared an excellent literature review from which much of the material of this chapter is drawn. I also thank Juan Antonio Montecino for his helpful comments on the material for this chapter and Chapter 5.

[3] "Key currency" countries are those that issue major international currencies.

[4] And as I discuss more fully below, Mitchell's contributions, as far as I have been able to tell, while useful are not extensive enough to guide policy support for MMT macroeconomic policies.

3.2 Sudden Stops and Speculative Exchange Rate Crises

Although I will be focusing in this chapter on more current episodes of reductions in fiscal space for developing countries, it is worth remembering that these problems of fiscal and monetary policy space plagued advanced European countries such as Italy in earlier times. In the 1960s, 1970s, and 1980s, Italy frequently had a balance of payments and exchange rate crises which interrupted fiscal and monetary expansions. This was true under both fixed exchange rates and managed floating regimes. While it is true that Italy, like most other countries, never adopted pure floating as Wray has recommended, an obvious question is why? As I discuss a little later in this chapter, "fear of floating" is usually sensible and rational for small open economies, especially highly indebted ones like Italy. One of the reasons Italy joined the Euro is because it calculated that (managed) floating exchange rates were either not viable or did not sufficiently create fiscal and monetary space. The same was true of many other sovereign currency countries in Europe. Hence, in Europe, we have many examples of countries with sovereign currencies that concluded that they could not achieve enough fiscal space in an integrated global economy with high degrees of capital mobility to achieve full employment.

3.3 Emerging Market Economies: The Extreme Difficulty of Pursuing MMT Policies in a Globally Financially Integrated World

Whatever difficulties the southern European countries and France had in launching full employment macroeconomic policies in the 1980s and 1990s, the problems confronting poor and emerging markets—even those with sovereign currencies—is far greater. Countries with open capital markets are subject to hot money inflows and outflows, surges and "sudden stops" (see, for example, Akyüz 2017). Surges, or "hot money inflows" are associated with increased liabilities on the balance sheets of local borrowers, instability in exchange rates, and difficulties managing liquidity conditions. Such inflows can often lead to overvalued exchange rates, current account deficits, and then rapid capital outflows and sudden stops, leaving local financial institutions and businesses with debts that are hard to service and repay (see Taylor 1991, chap. 6 for a classic model of this cycle).

These problems are exacerbated for countries that are not able to borrow internationally in their own currencies.[5] In this case, when capital flies out and the exchange rate depreciates, the local value of international debt increases, making it difficult for institutions in these countries to service their debts. Such excessive debts can have damaging impacts on investment, productivity, and employment. It can also lead to bankruptcies. There is substantial empirical evidence in support of these channels and problems. Eichengreen et al. (2005, 16) demonstrate that developing countries are much more volatile in their capacity to service their debt compared to advanced countries. If a country's debt is denominated, let us say in US dollars, its capacity to service its debt will depend on the value of its GDP in US dollars. Given the volatility of exchange rates (which is typically between 2 to 3 times higher in developing countries), a typical developing country with these constraints would face volatility of around 13% whereas a developed country without them would face volatility of around 2.7% per annum. Eichengreen et al. (2005) further argue that the volatility of the real exchange rate is not a concern only for short-term debt. The authors document that the volatility of movements in the five-year moving average of the real multilateral exchange rate is also very high; indeed, it moves for more than 60% in an average developing country. Hausmann (2004) shows that countries unable to borrow in their own currencies have lower evaluations of solvency as it intensifies the dependence of debt service on the movements of the exchange rate, which may be subject to crises and crashes due to its volatility. Further empirical evidence on the ability to borrow abroad in local currency is presented by Hausmann et al. (2001) and Bordo and Flandreau (2001). These two papers document that the set of countries that can borrow internationally in their domestic currency is quite limited, mainly to G-3 countries, with a few surprises such as Poland, South Africa, and Taiwan. The Bank for International Settlements (BIS) similarly documents that outstanding international debt securities are denominated in only four currencies, namely the US dollar, the pound sterling, the Euro and the Japanese Yen (quoted in Jeanneret and Souissi 2016, 202). No matter what the underlying cause is, the prevalence of high-interest rates limits fiscal expansions by lowering the sustainability of even *domestic* debt issued in the country's own sovereign currency. Indeed, there is significant evidence that most developing countries are unable to issue domestic cur-

---

[5] For some strange reason, the mainstream of the economics profession refers to this state of affairs as "original sin": a bizarre practice of blaming the victim dressed up in biblical garb.

rency debt at reasonably low interest rates. Most of the time, developing country governments have to offer high yields to make their bonds more attractive, even in their own countries. For instance, an IMF study shows that in a sample of 65 low-income countries, domestic debt, which only represent 21% of total debt absorbs 42% of the total interest bill. There is the further problem of fiscal procyclical fiscal policy in developing countries.

Procyclical fiscal policies are often attributed to difficulties of obtaining credit during recessions. Countercyclical policies require countries to issue debt when it is expensive to do so and to retire debt at a time when it is cheap to borrow (Panizza 2007; see also Aizenman et al. 2019).

3.4 Do Flexible Exchange Rates Provide the Solution?

As we have seen, Wray (2012) argues that the solution to these problems for developing countries with sovereign currencies is to adopt flexible exchange rates. But flexible exchange rates do not appear to work any better in developing and emerging economies than they did in vulnerable European countries in the 1980s and 1990s. There is an enormous literature on the issue of the possible insulation properties of flexible exchange rates. This literature is not uniform. Some empirical studies suggest that flexible exchange rates do provide some insulation properties for developing countries (see, for example, Klein and Shambaugh 2015). But even they find that this protection is far from complete. The preponderance of evidence, on the other hand, is that, in the age of massive capital flows and financial openness, flexible exchange rates provide very little, if any, monetary or fiscal policy autonomy or insulation properties for developing countries and emerging markets (see, for example, Montecino 2018; Hofmann and Takats 2015). Jorda et al. (2018) study the issue over a long time span and find that financial fluctuations emanating from global financial markets generate significant instability in developing countries. Looking over 150 years of history they find that "these fluctuations are transmitted across both fixed and floating exchange rate regimes, but the effects are more muted in floating exchange rate regimes." Focusing on the more recent period of high capital mobility and open capital markets, Rey (2015) and others find that the exchange rate regime has very little impact on providing policy autonomy for developing countries.In short, flexible exchange rates are no panacea for MMT policy in the developing world—not even close.

3.5 Capital Controls

Heterodox economists have argued for decades that in a highly financialized global economy, nations are likely to have to use multiple tools to manage the inflows and outflows of capital in order to maintain financial stability, full employment and to engage in sufficient long-term social investment to make crucial economic transitions. John Maynard Keynes, as James Crotty brilliantly shows, made capital controls a key component of his macroeconomic plans for full employment (Crotty 2019).

More recently, numerous heterodox economists, including Epstein et al. (2003), Chang and Grabel (2014), Gallagher et al. (2011), and even economists at the IMF (see Grabel 2017) have argued for the usefulness of capital controls (variously called "Capital Account Regulations," "Capital Management Techniques," and related names) to protect countries and their macroeconomic policies from the vagaries of global finance.

William Mitchell, an Australian Economist and major MMT figure, has written a number of pieces about capital controls. Perhaps it is fitting that an economist from a small open economy, and not the US, would see the importance of capital account regulations for small open economies (see, for example, Mitchell 2016; Mitchell and Fazi 2017). In his 2016 blog piece, entitled, *"Why Capital Controls Should Be Part of Progressive Policy"* Mitchell gives a summary of some of the evolution in thinking about the IMF on capital controls (see Grabel 2017 for a full discussion). Mitchell argues that capital controls can help to achieve more national sovereignty to pursue full employment and other progressive policies. In his book with Thomas Fazi, *"A Progressive Vision of Sovereignty for a Post Liberal World,"* Mitchell and Fazi reiterate the argument that such controls are an important part of the progressive policy tool kit.

These perspectives are a welcome deviation from the dominant MMT macroeconomic argument that flexible exchange rates will suffice to achieve macroeconomic autonomy for many if not most countries.

But several aspects are wanting in Mitchell's (and Fazi's treatment). As the large amount of heterodox (and recent IMF analysis) has shown for several decades, the details and institutional specificity of capital controls matters tremendously. If these were really an important component of an MMT approach to macroeconomic policy, MMT theorists and students would take the vast library of experiences, debates and lessons more seriously, and even contribute their own empirical analysis to understanding what works to support MMT style policy in different contexts. But this apparently is not on the MMT research agenda.

Instead, despite Mitchell's modest attention to the issue of capital controls in his blog piece and his book with Fazi, their book's introduction closes with this sweeping statement about MMT: "Fully embracing a progressive vision of sovereignty also means abandoning the many false macroeconomic myths that plague left-wing and progressive thinkers. One of the most pervasive and persistent myths is the assumption that governments are revenue-constrained, that is, that they need to 'fund' their expenses through taxes or debt. This leads to the corollary that governments have to 'live within their means', since ongoing deficits will inevitably result in an 'excessive' accumulation of debt, which in turn is assumed to be 'unsustainable' in the long run. In reality, as we show in Chapter 8, monetarily sovereign (or currency-issuing) governments – which nowadays include most governments – are never revenue-constrained because they issue their own currency by legislative fiat and always have the means to achieve and sustain full employment and social justice. In this sense, a progressive vision of national sovereignty should aim to reconstruct and redefine the national state as a place where citizens can seek refuge 'in democratic protection, popular rule, local autonomy, collective goods and egalitarian traditions'." (Mitchell and Fazi 2017, 13)

This is a nice vision, but no serious analysis of capital controls would show that they are sufficient to deliver this vision of free lunch accumulation of debt for countries outside a handful of hard currency countries, and probably not even most of them. To help emerging market and developing countries deal with the massive waves of international capital that buffet their economies, a more detailed and country-specific analysis of capital management techniques is required.

References

Aizenman, Joshua, Yothin Jinjarak, Hien Thi Kim Nguyen, and Donghyun Park. 2019. "Fiscal Space and Government-Spending and Tax-Rate Cyclicality Patterns: A Cross-Country Comparison, 1960–2016." *Journal of Macroeconomics* 60 (June): 229–252.

Akyüz, Yilmaz. 2017. *Playing with Fire: Deepened Financial Integration and Changing Vulnerabilities of the Global South.* Oxford: Oxford University Press.

Bordo, Michael, and Marc Flandreau. 2001. "Core, Periphery, Exchange Rate Regimes, and Globalization." w8584. Cambridge, MA: National Bureau of Economic Research.

Chang, Ha-Joon, and Ilene Grabel. 2014. *Reclaiming Development: An Alternative Economic Policy Manual*. London: Zed Books.

Crotty, James. 2019. *Keynes Against Capitalism: His Economic Case for Liberal Socialism*. Economics as Social Theory, 1st ed. New York: Routledge.

Eichengreen, Barry, Ricardo Hausmann, and Ugo Panizza. 2005. "The Pain of Original Sin." *Other People's Money: Debt Denomination and Financial Instability in Emerging Market Economies*. Chicago: University of Chicago Press.

Epstein, Gerald, Ilene Grabel, and Jomo K. S. 2003. "Capital Management Techniques in Developing Countries." In *Challenges to the World Bank and IMF; Developing Country Perspectives*, edited by Ariel Buira. London: Anthem Press.

Gallagher, Kevin P., Stephany Griffith-Jones, and Jose Antonio Ocampo. 2011. "Capital Account Regulations for Stability and Development: A New Approach." Boston University, Pardee Center, Issue Brief.

Grabel, Ilene. 2017. *When Things Don't Fall Apart: Global Financial Governance and Developmental Finance in an Age of Productive Incoherence*. Cambridge, MA: MIT Press.

Hausmann, Ricardo, Ugo Panizza, and Ernesto Stein. 2001. "Why Do Countries Float the Way They Float?" *Journal of Development Economics* 66 (2): 387–414.

Hausmann, Ricardo. 2004. "Good Credit Ratios, Bad Credit Ratings: The Role of Debt Structure." In *Rules-Based Fiscal Policy in Emerging Markets*, edited by George Kopits, 30–52. London, UK: Palgrave Macmillan.

Hofmann, Boris, and Elod Takats. 2015. "International Monetary Spillovers." *BIS Quarterly Review* (September): 105–118.

Jeanneret, Alexandre, and Slim Souissi. 2016. "Sovereign Defaults by Currency Denomination." *Journal of International Money and Finance* 60: 197–222.

Jorda, Oscar, Moritz Schularick, Alan M. Taylor, and Felix Ward. 2018. "Global Financial Cycles and Risk Premiums." NBER Working Paper No. 24677, June.

Klein, Michael W., and Jay C. Shambaugh. 2015. "Rounding the Corners of the Policy Trilemma: Sources of Monetary Policy Autonomy." *American Economic Journal: Macroeconomics* 7 (4): 33–66.

Mitchell, Bill. 2016. "Why Capital Controls Should Be Part of a Progressive Policy." Bill Mitchell's Blog, July 6, Wednesday.

Mitchell, William, and Thomas Fazi. 2017. *Reclaiming the State: A Progressive Vision of Sovereignty for a Post-liberal World*. London: Pluto Press.

Montecino, Juan Antonio. 2018. "International Strategic Spillovers of Monetary Policy." Columbia University.

Panizza, Ugo. 2007. "Is Domestic Debt the Answer to Debt Crises?" Columbia University.

Rey, Hélène. 2015. "Dilemma Not Trilemma: The Global Financial Cycle and Monetary Policy Independence." w21162. Cambridge, MA: National Bureau of Economic Research.

Taylor, Lance. 1991. *Income Distribution, Inflation and Growth; Lectures on Structuralist Macroeconomic Theory.* Cambridge, MA: MIT Press.

Wray, L. Randall. 2012. *Modern Money Theory: A Primer on Macroeconomics for Sovereign Monetary Systems.* London: Palgrave Macmillan.

CHAPTER 4

The Role of the Dollar as an International Currency and Its Limits in a Multi-Key Currency World

Abstract The United States, as the dominant issuer of the internationally accepted reserve currency, has the most ability to implement MMT style fiscal and monetary policy of all nations in the world. How secure is this role and how much can it be exploited? Major MMT figures, such as Randall Wray have argued that this role is so secure and exploitable that "we do not have to worry about it in our lifetimes". This chapter explores this question theoretically, empirically and historically. I conclude that the world is moving to a multi-currency system that will make that role less exploitable by MMT style macro-policy.

Keywords Key currency · Exorbitant privilege · Chinese Renminbi

4.1 Introduction

In the previous chapter I argued that the MMT approach to macro policy is not feasible for developing countries and that, in a highly financialized global financial system, flexible exchange rates will not substantially alter this verdict. Capital account regulations can help these countries reach domestic policy goals; however, they may not be sufficient to completely insulate these countries from the vagaries of international capital flows in the long run.

But for the United States and other large, wealthy countries, and especially those with internationally accepted currencies, the fiscal and monetary space is much greater. This is especially true for the United States which issues the predominant global currency, the US dollar. During the financial crisis of 2007–2009, the importance of this role for US fiscal and monetary policy was dramatically evident: when the US implemented a large fiscal expansion accompanied by extremely loose monetary policy, international capital poured into US dollar assets, lowering interest rate even further and appreciating the US exchange rate. This is a far cry from the market reactions to expansionary policies during recessions by developing and emerging market economies where there might be significant capital flight, depreciations of the exchange rate and increases in interest rates.

Still, the global financial consequences of a sustained MMT style policy could be significant. The financial and debt accumulation implications of MMT policy for the US is likely to be as follows: under this policy, the Federal Reserve would keep interest rates low indefinitely which, given the dynamics of domestic and global banking institutions and financial markets, would flood the global economy with dollar assets and liabilities strewn across the balance sheets of private and public institutions around the world. The expansionary macroeconomic policy would pull in imports and likely substantially increase the US current account deficit. Inflation would likely ratchet up. The dollar exchange rate could become more variable. These dynamics would raise "red flags" for global dollar holders and investors.

To what extent will the international role of the dollar sustain wealth holders' demand for dollars and prevent a flight from the dollar with its consequent increase in interest rates and possible fall in the exchange rate, as would surely happen under a similar policy regime in other countries? Will these limitations be avoided as US macroeconomic policy "exploits" the dollar's international role? Or, are there limits to the degree to which MMT fiscal and monetary policy can exploit the international role of the dollar? Are there economic limits to which the Fed can effectively print money to maintain low interest rates in a financially globalized world even with the dollar's mighty international role? What are those limits? How costly would it be to violate these limits?

In short, how sustainable is the dollar's international role?

These are important questions for an assessment of the long-term viability of MMT macro policy in the one country that provides the best opportunity for MMT viability, the US. We do not have precise answers (e.g., one cannot identify a precise threshold), but history and analysis do provide some useful parameters. The historical, theoretical and empirical research suggests that there is quite a bit of stability and persistence in key currencies' roles, but this persistence is not absolute. When there are plausible rivals to the dollar's role, economically, militarily, diplomatically, and a desire to internationalize their currencies, then the stability of the major currency's role has tighter limits than when there are no rivals in this sense. As I discuss below, in the current international environment there are two plausible rivals to the dollar, each with its own problems and potentials: The Euro and the Chinese Renminbi. While neither of these currencies is likely to overtake the US dollar as the dominant currency, their substantial existence means that we are likely to have a multicurrency international system. In such a world of currency competition, substitution among currencies in international transactions and portfolios is cheaper, easier and safer and this competition, like any competition, places limits on the price, stability, and general behavior of the dominant currency, the US dollar.

4.2 The "Exorbitant Privilege"

A country that is able to print a currency that is broadly accepted for payment internationally experiences an advantage, effectively extending monetary sovereignty to the international sphere. Furthermore, being able to issue international debt denominated in your own currency extends those advantages because it makes it possible to service and even repay that debt simply by printing money rather than having to run a trade surplus or borrow more from foreign institutions. These are benefits that accrue to countries that issue "hard currencies." Countries whose currencies are not acceptable in these ways are said to issue "soft currencies" (Epstein 2019, introduction).

Nevertheless, as we saw in the previous chapter, even for countries that issue hard currencies in this sense, many are subject to strong waves of turbulence from the international financial markets that can lead to fickle flows of short-term and even long-term capital in response to perceived weaknesses in countries' exchange rates, or changes in domestic interest rates that seem out of line with "international interest rates." In short, even for many "hard currency" countries, central banks, and fiscal authorities can be highly constrained in their policies even *before* they get to full employment. In these countries, effectively, MMT policies do not apply. For soft currency countries, the problems are much more severe.

But what about those countries that set, or have the major influence over international interest rates? Are they in a different boat? The answer is yes. They have more freedom to apply MMT type policies. The question is: to what extent and with what limits?[1]

These countries are known as "key" currency countries. Their currencies are used extensively internationally for all the standard functions of money plus some exclusively international functions: unit of account (invoicing currency, denomination of derivatives, denomination of bond and equity issues), intervention and anchor currency (intervenes in foreign exchange markets to limit fluctuations in value vis a vis that currency), store of value (held in international foreign exchange reserves, safe heaven holdings), medium of exchange (buying goods and services), means of payment (servicing debt), as a funding currency (to engage in arbitrage and speculation) and relatedly, as a means of collateral for liquidity and speculative transactions in the shadow finance system.

Of course, the currency that is most widely used in global markets and official portfolios is the US dollar. Far behind the dollar are the Euro, the Japanese Yen, the British pound, and the Chinese Renminbi. How valuable is this role for the US? In particular, to what extent does it mean that the US can apply MMT money financing of government spending, without tears?

Charles de Gaulle resented the role the US dollar played after the Bretton Woods system was established. His finance minister, Valery Giscard d'Estaing referred to it as "an exorbitant privilege" (Eichengreen 2011, 4). Jacques Rueff, a major economic adviser to De Gaulle put it this way: "If I had an agreement with my tailor that whatever money I pay him he returns to me the very same day as a loan, I would have no objection at all to ordering more suits from him" (as quoted in McCauley 2015, 2). As McCauley notes: the Gaullist view is that, under the Bretton Woods system, "not disciplined to settle debts, the US exploited the 1960's gold-exchange standard to buy goods, services and whole companies with US dollar IOUs" (ibid.), which, in theory, they never had to pay back.

Though the situation has changed since the collapse of Bretton Woods including the lack of compulsion on foreign countries now to hold dollars to fix their exchange rates relative to gold (and implicitly, the dollar), many of these structural advantages remain.

---

[1] Wray recognizes that, to some extent, the US is a special case (Wray 2012, 133).

Both Eichengreen and McCauley list the types of privileges the US receives under the current system and estimate their value (Eichengreen 2011, 4–5; McCauley 2015).
These privileges include[2]:

1. The US need not settle its dollar liabilities with some other asset.
2. The US can finance its current account deficits in its own currency.
3. The US runs up a debt at very low interest rates with the rest of the world.
4. The US treasury can borrow cheaply.
5. US financial firms harvest advantages (denomination rents) from global dollar use.
6. The US Fed has a big influence over global financial conditions and interest rates.
7. The US dollar is a safe-haven which helps to insulate US interest rates.[3]

Note that advantages 1–3 look very much like the characteristics of sovereign money as identified by MMT, but as a key currency, these are extended to the international arena.

Eichengreen, McCauley, and others have attempted to quantify these impacts, some of which are relevant here and discussed more below. The most relevant for our discussion are points 1, 2, 3, 4, 6 and 7. It is not hard to see that, to the extent that these are true and quantitatively important, they create space for the US government to issue more sovereign debt without risking an explosion of debt to GDP ratios, and allow the Federal Reserve to establish low interest rates despite this increase in debt, without

[2] There might be other benefits as well, such as the ability of local US firms to access global capital markets because their debt is denominated in dollar and they do not have to pay the costs of hedging or otherwise bear exchange rate risk (see Maggiori et al. 2018). Note that there might be costs of issuing an international currency as well, such as overvalued exchange rates. We ignore these because they are not germane to the main focus of the paper.

[3] Points 6 and 7 are not included in the lists created by Eichengreen or McCauley but are potentially important and relevant to the issues discussed in this paper. McCauley (2015) argues that most of these benefits, to the extent that they exist at all, are either shared with other currencies or are relatively small. The claim that many are shared with other key currencies is certainly true, but not important for the question of limits on MMT policies which is the focus here. The argument that they are small is more relevant, though disputed by other authors.

risking to the same extent as otherwise a foreign exchange crisis or negative feedback effect driving up interest rates in the US.

4.3 How Durable Is the Dollar's Role?

What are the limits on this debt creation and debt monetization process by the Fed? At one level, this question comes down to the question of how persistent and durable is the key currency role? This question in turn depends on the answer to another question: what determines the key currency role?

There is a huge literature on this topic, spanning many decades (see, for example, Kindleberger 1970; Bergsten 1973; Epstein 1981; Krugman 1984; Kirschner 1995; Prem 1997; Cohen 2015; Eichengreen 2011, 2019 and the vast literature cited therein).

Taken as a whole, the literature has focused on five key factors:

1. The so-called economic "fundamentals" of key currencies which are primarily driven by breadth, depth, and liquidity of the financial markets and the economic size of the economy.
2. The political and legal "fundamentals": the commitment to open markets in trade and finance, and the commitment to the rule of law and property rights (in short, the commitment to capitalist principles of property rights).
3. High levels of macroeconomic "policy credibility." Here, policy credibility refers to a commitment to relatively low and stable inflation, exchange rate stability, and monetary policy stability. This credibility can be established by past practice, and or by institutions which are likely to convince investors of these commitments, such as "independent" central banks. Commitment to "sustainable" sovereign debt levels would fall under this category.
4. Economic principles that generate persistence or dominance (monopoly): some have argued that phenomena such as network effects, economies of scale, and fixed costs and increasing returns to scale create persistence effects and first mover advantages that allow a currency to remain a key currency and even a dominant currency even after its fundamentals wane. If these effects are important, then MMT style policies are more likely to be sustainable and effective (Krugman 1984).
5. Military and diplomatic power: while most economists focus on economic issues noted in points 1–4 above, historians, political scientists,

policy observers, and some economists note the coincidence between countries that have strong military power and dense political and diplomatic alliances, and the maintenance of key currency role. Some economists have pointed out that military and diplomatic power can substitute to some extent for some of the other factors, including policy credibility, and trade prowess (see, for example, Prem 1997; Cohen 2015; Eichengreen et al. 2017).

Various analysts have undertaken econometric analyses of the determinants of the key currency roles (see Prem 1997; Eichengreen et al. 2017, 2018; Chinn and Frankel 2007, 2008). There are major empirical challenges to answering these questions. First of all, data on demand for international currencies is spotty and limited. Second, the number of key currencies in the mix are relatively small, so the number of data points is sparse.

All the empirical difficulties aside, there are useful results that come from the body of empirical work on this issue (see Eichengreen et al. 2017, 2018 for surveys and Prem 1997). The size of the economy, the breadth and depth of domestic financial markets, and extensiveness of trade networks are robust determinants of demand for the key currency.

The so-called credibility variables—inflation, budget deficits or debt ratios, and exchange rate variability generate mixed results. They usually operate in the expected direction but tend not to be statistically robust. This might be because countries that have been able to accumulate a significant key currency role based on large and deep financial markets also have political coalitions dominated by finance and are associated with "independent central banks" aligned with finance. This underlying political structure might underpin both the key currency role and the tight control over inflation and budget deficits (Epstein 1981).

One reason why the credibility factors might not be as robustly important as typically thought is related to a more general phenomenon: The evidence just described also suggest persistence in key currency role: that is, even if some of these economic factors, such as credibility, relative economic size, and trade signal a decline, the key currency role is sustained. In other words, considering the decline in the relative size of the US economy compared with that of China, the rise of Europe as a unified actor in this space and the relative size of Japan, the US dollar appears to punch above its weight. What accounts for this?

Possible answers include: the importance of military and diplomatic power, persistence due to network and related effects, and the evolution of new roles for the dollar in light of innovations in global financial markets and trade. The latter include the role of derivatives, safe assets, and global supply chains, including the role of US multinational corporations, and the rise of currency zones.

Prem (1997) was the first to show econometrically the important role of relative military power in preserving the key currency role. Eichengreen et al. (2017) provide strong evidence for the important role of political alliances and other diplomatic infrastructures. According to these analyses, a key currency country can to some extent, sustain its key currency role, even in the face of declining power of "economic" and "credibility" factors, by enhancing military and diplomatic pressures in the service of maintaining the international demand for the currency. We know, for example, that during the time of the Empire, the United Kingdom required that India hold its rupee balances in the form of pound sterling rather than cashing them in for gold, in order to help Britain stay on the gold standard (De Cecco 1975). Likewise, we know that the US applied pressure on the Germans to hold more dollar balances than they wanted, threatening to reduce US military protection against the Soviet Threat (Bergsten 1973).[4] In some cases, holders of key currencies might also prefer that the key currency have a strong military in order to protect the underlying property rights and the economy from political threats.

Of course, the effectiveness of this relative military and diplomatic power falls as new military and diplomatic powers rise. The current conflicts between the US and China reflect some of the tensions involved here and suggest that the US dominance is no longer as assured on this front as it once was. As this evolves, the ability for the US to "substitute" military power for "credibility," trade prowess and other "fundamentals" is likely to weaken. Likewise, Donald Trump's weakening of US global diplomatic ties is unlikely to enhance these supports for the international role of the dollar.

Another possible explanation for persistence in the face of "fundamentals" decline is network effects, economies of scale and fixed costs (Eichengreen et al. 2011, 2018). As Eichengreen et al. explain, some of these factors tend to generate monopolization of the key currency role, while other versions generate persistence but accommodate the presence of multiple key currencies. Eichengreen argues strongly for the latter and historical observation strongly suggests that he is right: leadership is persistent but

---

[4]This smacks of a kind of "vassal" tribute the master extracts through actual or implied force.

not assured, and at any moment there is certainly room for multiple and competitive players in the key currency space.

As Krugman showed decades ago (Krugman 1984) some network and economies of scale arguments for persistence also have a dramatic feature: they generate a tipping point so that fundamentals can decline for a while without generating any reduction in key currency role; but at a certain point, a marginal additional decline in fundamentals can cause a dramatic decline in key currency usage with all the attendant consequences.

Unfortunately, it is difficult to test this empirically. We have only had one major switch of leadership in the last century and a half: from the pound sterling to the US dollar. This doesn't provide many data points. However, it has been suggested that after years of decline by Sterling following the second World War, there was a fast and sharp unraveling following the Suez crisis of 1956. Similarly, in the run-up to the Great Financial Crisis, the Euro seemed to be gaining significant ground on the dollar (Chinn and Frankel 2007). But with the financial crisis followed by the Euro sovereign debt crisis, this rise of the Euro was stopped in its tracks and partially reversed (Eichengreen et al. 2018). So, there is some evidence of dramatic changes in response to shocks, suggesting some kinds of persistence effects that can quickly unravel.

Another important source of persistence is the role of "currency zones" or areas where countries anchor their currency values to the US dollar (Ito and McCauley 2018). As Ito and McCauley show, the size of the US currency zone relative to world GDP is much larger than the size of the US economy, and that the current account deficit of the zone is much smaller than of the US per se. In other words, if key currency "fundamentals" are measured by currency zone rather than by country, US key currency fundamentals are quite strong, which reduces the puzzle over the persistence of the international role of the dollar. It also suggests that, all else equal, the key currency role is likely to be more robust to the erosion of US "credibility" in the face of some inflation and increase in government debt ratios, in short to MMT type policies.

Looking at this broader picture, how robust is the dollar currency zone? Again, a lot depends on the role of China, the China–US relationship, and the decisions made by the Chinese government. A big chunk of the dollar zone consists of China. As Ito and McCauley show, if China leaves the dollar zone, then the dollar zone shrinks considerably, thereby increasing the importance of other factors supporting the dollar's key role, such as military power and market "credibility."

4.4 MMT AND THE ROLE OF THE DOLLAR: THE UPSHOT

What then is the upshot of this discussion for the question at hand: does the key currency role of the dollar enhance the effectiveness of MMT style policy? It almost certainly does. Can too much of this policy undermine the key currency role and generate a negative feedback effect on the viability of such policies? The answer is almost certainly: yes.

The real answer is that no one can know for sure. Those who argue that theory, history, and other evidence show that the dollar's staying power is absolute are certainly incorrect: From the false start of the dollar in the early twentieth century, to the decline of sterling, to the rapid decline of the Euro following the global financial crises, there is plenty of movement up and down in key currency roles in the course of history to disabuse any talk of invincibility. This fragility is particularly true when a "rival" to the dollar—namely China's Renminbi—exists that currently has most of the requirements to play that role: large trading role, huge foreign exchange reserves to give stability (much as the US gold stock provided for the US), a rising military and diplomatic presence in significant parts of the world, and a growing and liberalizing financial sector. Most important, is not only the apparent willingness on the part of the Chinese government to play a key currency role, but, it seems, a desire to do so. Analysts say that what is missing is deep and liquid financial markets, but that would not be hard for China to create once it decided to go all in.

Moreover, as Eichengreen has argued, one need not have a full switch from one key currency to another: the world is likely to live with a multicurrency system; this system need not necessarily be an unstable one, but it does provide more constraints and competition on each key currency. Hence, exploiting the "exorbitant privilege" becomes more difficult without disruption.

Does this all mean that an MMT policy of money financed budget deficits would quickly be undermined by global flight from the dollar? This seems unlikely in the short run, as long as macroeconomic policy doesn't allow excessive, accelerating inflation. Still, the risks of this flight from the dollar increase as the Chinese shrink the dollar zone and build a Renminbi one. In other words, despite what Wray has argued, this is likely to become a concern in "our lifetime."

Nonetheless, all this begs a key question: even if the dollar's international role will help to protect the viability of a MMT path, is it responsible and right from an international perspective to follow this approach?

I address this question in the next chapter.

References

Bergsten, C. Fred. 1973. *The Dilemmas of the Dollar*. New York: New York University Press.

Chinn, Menzi, and Jeffrey Frankel. 2007. "Will the Euro Eventually Surpass the Dollar as Leading International Currency?" In *G7 Current Account Imbalances and Adjustment*, edited by Richard Clarida. Chicago: University of Chicago Press.

Chinn, Menzi, and Jeffrey Frankel. 2008. "Why the Euro Will Rival the Dollar." *International Finance* 11 (1), 49–73.

Cohen, Benjamin. 2015. *Currency Power: Understanding Monetary Rivalry*. Princeton, NJ: Princeton University Press.

De Cecco, Marcello. 1975. *Money and Empire: The International Gold Standard, 1890–1914*. Totowa, NJ: Rowman and Littlefield.

Eichengreen, Barry. 2011. *Exorbitant Privilege; The Rise and Fall of the Dollar and the Future of the International Monetary System*. Oxford: Oxford University Press.

Eichengreen, Barry, Arnaud Mehl, and Livia Chitu. 2017. "Mars or Mercury? The Geopolitics of International Currency Choice." NBER Working Paper No. 24145, December.

Eichengreen, Barry, Arnaud Mehl, and Livia Chitu. 2018. *How Global Currencies Work: Past, Present and Future*. Princeton, NJ: Princeton University Press.

Epstein, Gerald. 1981. "Domestic Stagflation and Monetary Policy: The Federal Reserve and the Hidden Election." In *The Hidden Election*, edited by Thomas Ferguson and Joel Rogers. New York: Pantheon Press, reprinted in: Gerald Epstein, *The Political Economy of Central Banking: Contested Control and the Power of Finance*. Northampton, MA: Edward Elgar, 2019.

Epstein, Gerald. 2019. *The Political Economy of Central Banking: Contested Control and the Power of Finance*. Northampton, MA: Edward Elgar Press.

Ito, Hiro, and Robert N. McCauley. 2018. "A Key Currency View of Global Imbalances." *SSRN Scholarly Paper ID 3329727*. Rochester, NY: Social Science Research Network. https://papers.ssrn.com/abstract=3329727.

Kindleberger, Charles P. 1970. *Power and Money; The Economics of International Politics and the Politics of International Finance*. New York: Basic Books.

Kirschner, Jonathan. 1995. *Currency and Coercion: The Political Economy of International Monetary Power*. Princeton: Princeton University Press.

Krugman, Paul. 1984. "The International Role of the Dollar: Theory and Prospect." In *Exchange Rate Theory and Practice*, edited by John Bilson and Richard Marston, 513–526. Chicago: University of Chicago Press.

Maggiori, Matteo, Brent Neiman, and Jesse Schreger. 2018. "International Currencies and Capital Allocation." NBER Working Paper No. 24673.

McCauley, Robert N. 2015. Does the US Dollar Confer an Exorbitant Privilege? *Journal of International Money and Finance* 57: 1–14.

Prem, Roohi. 1997. "International Currencies and Endogenous Enforcement—An Empirical Analysis." International Monetary Fund, Working Paper No. 29, March.

Wray, L. Randall. 2012. *Modern Money Theory: A Primer on Macroeconomics for Sovereign Monetary Systems*. London: Palgrave Macmillan.

CHAPTER 5

"America First" Monetary Policy and Its Costs

Abstract This chapter asks if the United States should pursue an MMT type monetary and fiscal policy even if it could, from the perspective of the emerging and developing countries. The chapter argues that while there might be some benefits for these countries, there could also be significant costs associated with floods and then sudden stops in capital flows, which can lead to significant macroeconomic problems for these countries. As a blueprint for a progressive macroeconomic policy, these impacts should be taken into account, including a more serious discussion of mitigating policies, such as financial regulations, capital controls and modifications in the US macro policy if necessary.

Keywords Monetary policy spillovers · Sudden stops · Hot money

5.1 INTRODUCTION

Even if an MMT low interest rate, expansionary deficit macroeconomic policy, accompanied by fiscal tightening at full employment, does not threaten the sustainability of US's "exorbitant privilege," it doesn't mean that this is an appropriate policy for the rest of the world. This is a US-centric macroeconomic policy. While it is true that US macroeconomic policy has usually been national-centric, that doesn't necessarily mean that this is the right

© The Author(s) 2019
G. A. Epstein, *What's Wrong with Modern Money Theory?*,
https://doi.org/10.1007/978-3-030-26504-5_5

policy for a progressive agenda. This "America First" policy does raise questions that should be of burning concern to progressives, especially those with an internationalist orientation. Would this policy inflict unjustified costs on other parts of the world, and especially the least powerful and wealthy parts? If so, should the policy be modified? Reversed? Augmented with other policies to mitigate the negative impacts?

There is a good reason to believe that this MMT oriented macro policy could create significant policy problems in other countries. Many of these spillover effects are caused by the dominant role that the US dollar plays in the global arena. Thus, these negative costs for others are, at least partly, a direct result of the very institutional arrangements that would help to sustain MMT policy at home. I argue that a more solidaristic US policy would be modified and/or be accompanied by compensatory or preventative policy reforms to mitigate these negative impacts. Unfortunately, there is no evidence that MMT advocates seriously consider, much less develop solutions to these potential negative spillover effects on the rest of the world. Fortunately, much of this analysis and research has been taken on by other heterodox economists and researchers for many years.

5.2 Hot Money Floods and Famines: Global Monetary and Financial Instability Emanating from the Federal Reserve and the Role of the Dollar

Developing country economies have always been subject to the vagaries of financial decisions made by "center" countries, including the United Kingdom and in later years, the United States (Kindleberger 1978). Diaz-Alejandro (1985) famously tied these center-induced financial crises to center countries' financial conditions and financial liberalization on the periphery. Epstein (1981), among others, identified the dramatic Volcker interest rate hikes as sending dangerous shockwaves that would generate financial crises in Latin America and abroad, causing significant problems for many economies. Thus, the financial conditions and monetary policy in the center countries have driven financial conditions in the periphery for decades, and this is especially true now.

A great deal of empirical research demonstrates that the multiple and leading international roles played by the dollar is a key channel through which the Federal Reserve monetary policy is a dominant force that spills over to the financial conditions in much of the rest of the global economy. These spillover effects impact the richer countries (see, for example, McCauley 2015) but their impacts are larger on so-called "emerging market" economies. At the same time, these economies have fewer tools for coping with these spillovers (Akyüz 2017; D'Arista 2019). As I discussed earlier, current research demonstrates that capital flow surges and sudden stops remain frequent and large vis a vis emerging markets and have major disruptive effects. Whereas the frequency in recent years is not larger than in the earlier ones, Eichengreen shows that the magnitude of the turnaround is larger and the negative impacts are more substantial as well in the later period. Declines in GDP with flow surges and sudden stops are now often of a larger magnitude than they were in the earlier period (Eichengreen and Gupta 2016).

What are the main causes of these surges and sudden stops? Current research points the finger largely at the policy of the US Federal Reserve as transmitted through the key, multiple roles of the dollar (Rey 2015; Eichengreen and Gupta 2016; Brauning and Ivashina 2018; Avdjiev et al. 2018; Jorda et al. 2018). Rey (2015) was among the first researchers to identify changes in risk perception as a driver of global financial conditions. She indicated that Fed policy had a particularly strong impact on these risk perceptions.[1] Eichengreen and Gupta show that these risk perceptions drive inflows and sudden stops in their sample. They also find evidence that changes in the Fed's Federal Funds rate also drives these flows.

Other recent research has identified the channels through which US monetary policy impact global financial conditions, and the "fingerprints" of the US dollar and US financial institutions are all over these flows. For example, in a study using detailed loan-level data on bank lending from 1990 to 2016, Brauning and Ivashina (2018) find that over 80% of cross-border loans to EMEs are denominated in US dollars. This high portion is common in most regions of the world. "Outstanding shares of foreign banks' dollar credit for African, American, and Asian emerging economies are over 90%. Even for emerging Europe this number is over 60 percent" (p. 28). They show that "this dollarization of cross-border credit prevails over time and across different geographic regions and industries" (p. 3). As a result, conclude Brauning and Ivashina, "U.S. monetary policy plays

---

[1] Typically, risk perception is measured by the VIX index in this literature.

an important role as a 'push factor' for credit cycles through its impact on US interest rates" (p. 3).

Brauning and Ivashina do a regression-based analysis to identify the specific effects of US monetary policy on bank lending to emerging markets both during periods of easing and tightening, relative to the impacts on developed market economies. They estimate that over a "typical US monetary easing cycle, EME borrowers experience a 32 percentage point greater increase in the volume of loans issued by foreign banks than do borrowers from developed markets, followed by a fast credit contraction of a similar reversal of the US monetary policy stance…(They also) show that the spillover is stronger for risker EMEs, and, within countries, for higher risk firms (ibid., 1). These results help to illustrate how spillover effects of Fed policy, through bank lending based on the US dollar, can induce financial instability in emerging market economies" (see also Avdjiev et al. 2018).

This outsized impact of US monetary policy on macroeconomic conditions in the rest of the world, and especially in developing countries, would seem to call out for a more globally oriented monetary policy on the part of the Federal Reserve. At the minimum, it would suggest the need for consultation and cooperation between the Fed and other monetary authorities. But such coordination and cooperation are spotty, at best.[2]

Certainly, a progressive macroeconomic policy can do better than this, can it not?

5.3 Implications of Fed Spillover Effects for MMT Policy

MMT advocates' responses to these points might be as follows:

First, they could argue that a MMT policy of stable, low Fed interest rates and full employment fiscal policy would not amount to a "stop-go" macroeconomic policy that has generated so much instability in the rest of the world. On the contrary, they might argue, the MMT policy would amount to a steady as it goes policy that would minimize unstable global spillovers.

---

[2] During crises this cooperation and consultation tends to increase. The Federal Reserve's extensive international lender of last resort actions through extending swap lines and coordinated interest rate declines are cases in point; but most emerging and poor countries were not included or consulted in these actions.

Second, they could argue that a full employment expansionary policy with low interest rates would drive a global economic expansion on the demand side and would help to generate growth in developing countries. At first glance, both of these points have merit. But on deeper consideration, these points generate many questions that require careful analysis and further study.

First, is it really true that the MMT policy of keeping interest rates low and fiscal policy oriented to full employment, subject to an inflation constraint, amount to a stable policy? Palley, for example, has pointed out the difficulties of implementing such a fine-tuned policy, given lags in policy, uncertainty, and shocks, and the dynamic evolution of the economy such that policies can lose their effectiveness and predictable effects over time. (Palley 2019a, b). We simply do not know to what extent this kind of "fine-tuning" can succeed to stabilize the economy.

Second, there is a far larger problem that the MMT policy might engender, one that the MMT focus on sovereign money, and ignoring credit, leaves in the shadows: the possible impact of excessive private credit creation on financial speculation, bubbles and financial instability.

Numerous authors have identified the dynamic, instability inducing impacts of excessive private credit flows on domestic and international economies (Kindleberger 1978; D'Arista 2019). There is considerable evidence that, with liberalized financial markets, long term low interest rates can generate a stretch for yield, leading to risky lending, and promote asset bubbles, which eventually crash (e.g., Schularick and Taylor 2010). In conjunction with liberalized financial markets, this low rate monetary policy also contributed to the housing speculation and crisis (Mian and Sufi 2018). Further evidence is found in the work of Jorda et al. (2018) who look at the factors driving global financial cycles with a data set that spans 150 years and 17 "advanced capitalist" countries. They find that extended periods of low interest rates appear to contribute to an increase in risk-taking and can contribute to financial instability. They find that it is "fluctuations in risk premiums....that account for a large part of the observed (global) equity price synchronization after 1990....(they) also show that U.S. monetary policy has come to play an important role as a source of fluctuations in risk appetite across global equity markets."

In short, MMT policy of very low long term interest rates and full employment fiscal policy might contribute to increases in speculative lending, asset bubbles and financial instability, both in the US and, given the international role of the dollar, to many other parts of the world. Note that these negative impacts come even from steady as you go, very low Fed interest rates in a financially liberalized and integrated world.

This does not necessarily mean that low interest rates are bad. But it does suggest that key complementary policies, such as financial regulations, capital controls, and credit allocating central banks are likely to be an important accompaniment to such policies if they are to avoid destabilizing the economy.

5.4 Mitigating Possible Negative Impacts of MMT Macroeconomic Policy

Can anything be done to ameliorate these negative effects?

The answer is: presumably yes. Fortunately, heterodox economists, and, increasingly, mainstream economists, have been studying policy options facing emerging markets and others which would allow them to manage such problems. Ocampo (2017), Epstein et al. (2003), Chang and Grabel (2014), Gallagher et al. (2011), and Erten and Ocampo (2017) among others have extensively studied how developing countries can insulate themselves from dangers emanating for center country monetary and macroeconomic policy, focusing on capital management techniques, Tobin Taxes, and other capital account regulations.[3] The IMF and BIS have recently built on this work and developed policies of prudential regulation (IMF 2018).[4] But US policy would have to support such initiatives. As Grabel (2017) shows, the US policy has been changing on these issues, but moves in fits and starts.

Going further, some Keynesians have long proposed that a global currency and central bank would eliminate exorbitant privileges (Stiglitz 2009). But pursuing this would involve giving up the dollar's exorbitant privilege, and thereby limit national MMT style policy in the US. In such a world, "America First" monetary policy would probably have to go.

---

[3] As I discussed earlier, William Mitchell has also discussed some of these issues (see, e.g. Mitchell 2016).

[4] Ilene Grabel has written a brilliant book on what see calls the "productive incoherence" of the IMF's changing views on capital controls and related topics (Grabel 2017).

REFERENCES

Akyüz, Yilmaz. 2017. *Playing with Fire: Deepened Financial Integration and Changing Vulnerabilities of the Global South.* Oxford: Oxford University Press.

Avdjiev, Stefan, Valentina Bruno, Catherine Koch, and Hyun Song Shin. 2018. "The Dollar Exchange Rate as a Global Risk Factor: Evidence from Investment." BIS Working Papers No. 695, January.

Brauning, Falk, and Victoria Ivashina. 2018. "U.S. Monetary Policy and Emerging Market Credit Cycles." NBER Working Paper No. 25185, October.

Chang, Ha-Joon, and Ilene Grabel. 2014. *Reclaiming Development: An Alternative Economic Policy Manual.* London: Zed Books.

D'Arista, Jane. 2019. *All Fall Down: Debt, Deregulation and Financial Crises.* Northampton: Edward Elgar.

Diaz-Alejandro, Carlos. 1985. "Good-Bye Financial Repression, Hello Financial Crash." *Journal of Development Economics* 19 (1–2): 1–24.

Eichengreen, Barry, and P. Gupta. 2016. "Managing Sudden Stops." Policy Research Paper No. 7639, World Bank.

Epstein, Gerald. 1981. "Domestic Stagflation and Monetary Policy: The Federal Reserve and the Hidden Election." In *The Hidden Election*, edited by Thomas Ferguson and Joel Rogers. New York: Pantheon Press, Reprinted in: Gerald Epstein, *The Political Economy of Central Banking: Contested Control and the Power of Finance.* Northampton, MA: Edward Elgar, 2019.

Epstein, Gerald, Ilene Grabel, and Jomo K. S. 2003. "Capital Management Techniques in Developing Countries." In *Challenges to the World Bank and IMF; Developing Country Perspectives*, edited by Ariel Buira. London: Anthem Press.

Erten, Bilge, and José Antonio Ocampo. 2017. "Macroeconomic Effects of Capital Account Regulations." *IMF Economic Review.* International Monetary Fund 65 (2) (June): 193–240.

Gallagher, Kevin P., Stephany Griffith-Jones, and Jose Antonio Ocampo. 2011. "Capital Account Regulations for Stability and Development: A New Approach." Boston University, Pardee Center, Issue Brief.

Grabel, Ilene. 2017. *When Things Don't Fall Apart: Global Financial Governance and Developmental Finance in an Age of Productive Incoherence.* Cambridge, MA: MIT Press.

IMF. 2018. "A Decade After the Global Financial Crisis: Are we Safer?" *Global Financial Stability Report 2018.* Washington, DC: IMF.

Jorda, Oscar, Moritz Schularick, Alan M. Taylor, and Felix Ward. 2018. "Global Financial Cycles and Risk Premiums." NBER Working Paper No. 24677, June.

Kindleberger, Charles P. 1978 and later editions. *Manias, Panics and Crashes.* New York: Basic Books.

McCauley, Robert N. 2015. "Does the US Dollar Confer an Exorbitant Privilege?" *Journal of International Money and Finance* 57: 1–14.

Mian, Atif, and Amir Sufi. 2018. "Credit Supply and Housing Speculation." NBER Working Paper No. 24823.

Mitchell, Bill. 2016. "Why Capital Controls Should Be Part of a Progressive Policy." Bill Mitchell's Blog, July 6, Wednesday.

Ocampo, Jose Antonio. 2017. *Resetting the International Monetary (Non)System*. WIDER Studies in Development Economics. Oxford: Oxford University Press.

Palley, Thomas I. 2019a. "What's Wrong with Modern Money Theory (MMT): A Critical Primer." Forum for Macroeconomics and Macroeconomic Policies No. 44, March.

Palley, Thomas I. 2019b. "Macroeconomics vs. Modern Money Theory: Some Unpleasant Keynesian Arithmetic." Post Keynesian Economics Society, Working Paper No. 1910, April.

Rey, Hélène. 2015. "Dilemma Not Trilemma: The Global Financial Cycle and Monetary Policy Independence." w21162. Cambridge, MA: National Bureau of Economic Research.

Schularick, Moritz, and Alan M. Taylor. 2010. "Credit Booms Gone Bust: Monetary Policy, Leverage Cycles and Financial Crises, 1870–2008". NBER Working Paper.

Stiglitz, Joseph. 2009. *Report of the Commission of Experts of the President of the United Nations General Assembly on Reforms of the International Monetary and Financial System*. New York: United Nations.

CHAPTER 6

The Mystery of the Missing Minsky: Financial Instability as a Constraint on MMT Macroeconomic Policy

Abstract There is a deep paradox in the MMT analysis: on the one hand, key MMT theorists like Randall Wray are followers (and experts) on the work of Hyman Minsky. They have also written extensively on financial instability and financial regulation. Yet, in the context of their MMT macroeconomic policies, they fail to address the potential financial instability dangers that might arise from these policies. I call this the *mystery of the missing Minsky*. The explanation for the paradox is that they assume that sovereign money, by definition, solves the financial instability problems laid out by Minsky. In my view, this represents a misreading of both Minsky and reality, especially in the context of modern, globalized, financial market structures.

Keywords Financial instability hypothesis · Safe assets · Reach for yield

6.1 Introduction

In previous chapters, I have argued that MMT's macroeconomic policy framework of permanently low (even *zero*) Federal Reserve policy interest rates, combined with debt-monetized fiscal spending, unconstrained by financial considerations, and only limited by a full capacity constraint, potentially has a number of financial dangers. These include the issues of inflation and exchange rate problems which might arise prior to full employ-

© The Author(s) 2019
G. A. Epstein, *What's Wrong with Modern Money Theory?*,
https://doi.org/10.1007/978-3-030-26504-5_6

ment and "Bond vigilantes" who, despite the existence of excess real capacity, rebel against the accumulation of public debt and drive longer term interest rates higher.

In previous chapters, I have also raised the concern that this policy could lead to financial bubbles, financial instability and financial crises as the permanently low interest rates and large global amount of increased available liquidity could lead to a buildup of risky financial investments, leverage, speculative financial flows and asset bubbles not just in the United States but in much of global economy; that the waves of dollar credit that could be unleashed could facilitate hot money flows, exchange rate speculation and debt problems for so-called emerging market countries and other developing economies; and that these self-propelling processes could lead to problems, not only for developing countries that attempt to implement MMT style macroeconomic policies, but also to even those that don't (see Chapters 3 and 5).

Yet, despite the historical and empirical evidence for such dangers that I noted in previous chapters, the major MMT theorists, with the possible exception of Bill Mitchell—who has written about the importance of capital controls—have not identified these processes as a significant potential limitation on the set of MMT macroeconomic policy proposals. Nor, for the most part, have MMTers emphasized the need to regulate the financial system to prevent such problems as an important complement to their debt monetized, fiscal expansion driven macro-policy. Yet, this lack of discussion of financial regulations in this context stands in stark contrast to their many discussions of financial regulation in other contexts.

In my view, this relative silence is profoundly paradoxical. It is a paradox because this self-reinforcing process of leverage accumulation, risky position taking, asset bubbles and financial instability is a core idea of one of MMT's main intellectual inspirations: Hyman Minsky. As I discuss in this chapter, the core idea of Hyman Minsky is the "financial instability hypothesis." This hypothesis is that, in a typical capitalist economy, a period of stability sets off a process of self-reinforcing forces that lead to the types of financial problems as I just described in the previous paragraph (Minsky 1972). While Minsky's work primarily focused on the US, the great MIT financial economic historian, Charles Kindleberger, inspired by Minsky's work, extended Minsky's work to the international arena in his classic book *Manias, Panics and Crashes* (1978). A long period of low to zero interest rates and full employment, for a number of reasons I explore below, should be especially prone to this kind of instability both in the US and, because of the key role of the dollar and the massive global footprint of the US financial system in the larger world.

In fact, the paradox is deeper because the main developers of MMT themselves are also experts—perhaps THE experts—on the work of Hyman Minsky. Randy Wray was a student of Minsky's and has written extensively on Minsky's work, including his work on financial instability. In fact, virtually all MMT writers are well versed in the basics and the nuances of Minsky's work. Yet in the context of MMT's signature macroeconomic policy proposals on debt monetization, low interest rate monetary and expansionary fiscal policy, as far as I can tell, they ignore these "financial instability" dangers.

In this chapter, I explore this *Mystery of the Missing Minsky*. My main argument is that the paradox is resolved by understanding the MMT theorists' misinterpretation of Minsky's argument on the relationship between government spending and financial instability and by their failure to adequately address major changes in the structure of global financial markets. Taking these two aspects into account help to resolve the mystery and also point to the need to take into account financial reforms to complement MMT macro policy.

Fortunately, as I discuss in the following section, some MMT analysts are developing important, relevant work on this topic. Nersisyan and Dantas (2017), for example, have done significant work trying to incorporate international shadow banking considerations into MMT theory and policy and their implications for policy. I conclude that further development of these approaches would likely enhance the credibility and viability of MMT style macroeconomic policy.

6.2 Hyman Minsky and the Financial Instability Hypothesis

Numerous authors have offered useful expositions of Hyman Minsky's Financial Instability Hypotheses including Randall Wray (e.g., Tymoigne and Wray 2014), Gary Dymski and Robert Pollin (1992), Eric Tymoigne (2009) and, of course, Hyman Minsky himself (e.g., 1982, 1986). I will refer here mostly to Tymoigne and Wray's exposition since it is the work of the MMTers and their approach to Minsky which is the main topic of this chapter.

In the context of his discussion of financial instability, Minsky mostly emphasizes the role of finance in facilitating the acquisition of long-term capital assets by business and households. In his later work, Minsky recognizes that, in the case of modern financial systems, this role has changed and that increasingly, finance also plays the role of financing speculative activity by the financial system itself. This point becomes crucial in the argument that follows. The financial system facilitates the acquisition of long term assets through the process of lending (and investing). In this regard, finance is thus crucial to economic growth. But it can also create problems.

Tymoigne and Wray (2014) state that "The main point of (Minsky's) framework is to show that during periods of economic stability, economic units make sensible economic decisions that push them to use more leverage and decrease the quality of this leverage while also engaging in more risky activities" (p. 249). Hence, according to Minsky: "Stability is de-stabilizing" (Minsky 1982). Why is this the case? Say Tymoigne and Wray: "The reason why stability is de-stabilizing has many roots but Minsky was convinced that the nature of the current economic system had a lot to do with it. Capitalism, with is growth-oriented and money-oriented focuses, is an unstable system" (p. 249).

More specifically, Minsky develops a schematic analysis of the process of using finance to acquire capital assets and the stages and processes which generate this instability. In particular, he developed a useful typology of financial positions that businesses, households, and financial firms ("units") could find themselves in. This famous trilogy is, in increasing degrees of precariousness, Hedge Finance, Speculative Finance and Ponzi Finance (Tymoigne and Wray, p. 190). In Minsky's scheme, all these units are solvent in principle (otherwise, say Tymoigne and Wray, banks would not lend to them). The key difference among the units is the degree to which their income is sufficient to finance their debt positions, and the degree to which they have to refinance their debt obligations—interest payments and or principle repayment obligations—because their assets are too illiquid to finance these payments without jeopardizing their positive net worth (ibid.).

According to Tymoigne and Wray (2014):

> **Hedge finance** means that an economic unit is expected to be able to meet its liability commitments with the net cash flow it generates from its routine economic operations (work for most individuals, going concern for companies) and monetary balances. …an economy in which most economic units rely on hedge finance is not prone to debt-deflation pro-

cesses...**Speculative finance** means that routine net cash-flow sources and monetary balances are expected to be high enough to be able to pay the income component (interest, dividend, annuities, among others) but too low to pay the capital component (debt principal, margin calls, cash withdrawals, and insurance payments, among others) of liabilities. As a consequence, an economic unit needs either to borrow funds or to sell some less-liquid assets to pay liability commitments. **Ponzi finance**...means that an economic unit is not expected to generate enough net cash flow from its routine economic operations, or to have enough liquid assets that can be converted into cash to pay the capital and income service due on outstanding financial contracts. As a consequence, Ponzi finance involves an expectation of borrowing money and/ or selling non-monetary assets in order to pay interest and principal payments on debts... At the macroeconomic level, if key economic units behind the growth of the economy are involved in Ponzi finance, the economic system is highly prone to a debt deflation. (pp. 22–23)

According to the financial instability hypothesis, the more Ponzi finance units there are in the economy, the more prone the economy is to a financial crisis.

Crucial for the emergence of these different types of financing positions for Minsky is the concept of "margins of safety." Banks and other lenders, as well as the borrowers themselves, build in margins of safety to make it more likely that their borrowers can service and ultimately pay back their loans (ibid., p. 194). When these are violated, then units will have to engage in "position-making," that is borrowing or liquidating nonliquid or critical assets.

Importantly, according to Tymoigne and Wray, these problems cannot be reduced to external funding or leverage per se.

...this categorization is not a measure of the use of external funding, i.e., of the size of leverage; but rather, a measure of the quality of the leverage. At the core of this analytical definition is an analysis of the financial means that are expected to be available for economic units in order to fulfill their financial contracts. The more an economic unit is expected to need defensive position-making operations, the more financially fragile it is. Position-making operations are portfolio transactions (buying/ selling assets, borrowing/ lending) induced by the existence of an excess or a shortage of cash relative to the needs of an economic unit. (p. 23)

Ponzi finance is particularly problematic.

> Ponzi finance is a financial position that is expected to require a growing use of position-making operations... More precisely, Ponzi finance relies on an expected growth of refinancing loans ..., and/ or an expected full liquidation of asset positions at growing asset prices...in order to meet debt commitments on a given level of outstanding financial contracts... Ponzi finance is an unsustainable financial process. Indeed, in order to persist it requires an exponential growth of financial participation, which is not possible because, ultimately, there is a limited number of economic agents that can or will participate. (p. 23).

The need for asset price appreciation as this develops is especially noteworthy.

> When position-making needs are growing, rising asset prices are a requirement in order to maintain the net worth of an economic unit and to allow the unit to refinance the same or a growing amount of outstanding debt. If asset prices decline and lead to a decline in net worth, bankers will refuse to rollover existing loans and will demand a bigger down payment given the loan-to-value ratio. (p. 24)

The key argument that Minsky makes is that, in a period of stability and tranquility, where most units are hedge, and banks are lending with large margins of safety, the forces that maintain this situation begin to erode and the economy inexorably moves to one where more and more firms become hedge and then Ponzi, and that lenders and borrowers tolerate smaller and smaller margins of safety. What, according to Minsky, are these forces? According to Minsky, there are longer term forces that begin in the period of stability and relative tranquility; and there are a second set of more speculative forces that join as the boom develops. As the economy grows, more units finance longer term assets, but because of the limitations in the growth of productivity, and a limited ability to squeeze workers' wages as capacity utilization rises, cash flow relative to commitments declines. Margins of safety also tend to decline as these processes accelerate. More units move toward speculative and then Ponzi positions.

All of this is accelerated in the boom period, the second process. Overly optimistic expectations become self-generating even to the point of euphoria, lenders too become overly optimistic and margins decline further, and units begin to depend more on future asset price appreciation to meet their commitments. A bust is just a matter of time. Tymoigne and Wray emphasize that these short term boom processes which for Minsky are critical, are nonetheless rooted in the longer term trend toward financial instability starting in the period of tranquility (pp. 24–27).

Tymoigne and Wray emphasize that there can be other forces in capitalism leading to financial crises: pure speculation, asset bubbles, fraud. This is important because the strict schematic of hedge/speculative/ponzi financing is only one channel through financial crises occur. In modern financial markets, as Tymoigne and Wray themselves discuss (2014) there are multiple processes that can lead to financial excess and crisis (see also Kindleberger 1978 and Tokunaga and Epstein (2018) for the international context). For example, Kindleberger, in his discussion of *Manias, Panics and Crashes*, notes the problem of speculation that often emerges in a period of low interest rates: "a search for yield," leading investors to take on more speculative and highly leveraged positions to earn a previously expected rate of return. As Kindleberger puts it, quoting Walter Bagehot: "*John Bull* can stand many things, but he *cannot* stand 2 percent" (Kindleberger 1978). Jane D'Arista has noted similar problems in her recent book (D'Arista 2019). Economists from the *Bank for International Settlements (BIS)* such as William White and Claudio Borio, for example, have warned of such dangers in the context of longer term low interest rates.

Thus, Minsky's Theory suggests that MMT macro policy of long term, low interest rate, debt monetized fiscal policy, might well set up some of these dangerous financial processes. Yet, MMTers mostly ignore this danger. Why?

6.3 The Mystery of the Missing Minsky

These processes just described seem to well-characterize the dynamics that could ensue if the MMT macroeconomic policy were to be implemented. Permanent very low to zero policy interest rate, long term government financed full employment it, appears, would lead to a movement in the economy from hedge to speculative to Ponzi positions, with added risks of speculative bubbles and risk-taking due to the processes that Kindleberger, among many others, describe. Yet, MMT theorists such as Randy Wray and Stephanie Kelton do not seem to discuss these dangers at all in the context of their proposed fiscal policies.

Why?

The reason appears to be found in combining some arguments of Minsky's on the financial impact of government spending, with the MMTers claims about sovereign money. Tymoigne and Wray write:

One should note that the (hedge/speculative/Ponzi) category does not apply to monetarily sovereign governments, i.e., governments that issue their own nonconvertible currency and securities denominated in their currency. Hedge finance applies to all sovereign government that issues its own currency. (2014, 24)

By this Tymoigne and Wray argue that Minsky's financial instability dynamic does not take place in the case of government spending funded by borrowing by sovereign governments because, by definition, these involve "hedge" financing. This is true, according to MMTers, because, by MMT definition, these governments cannot be forced into default.

In other words, the US government, no matter how large its debt or deficit, or how high-interest rates, is a hedge unit. In short, by definition, the financial instability hypothesis is ruled out for debt-financed government spending.

This MMT argument appears to be reinforced by a point made by Minsky himself: according to Minsky, when the federal government spends, it actually adds income and cash flow to businesses and households. As a result, all else equal, this spending ought to reduce the amount of speculative and ponzi financing in the private sector. Yet all else is not equal; this argument ignores the important distinction between financial instability due to classic, stylized Minsky processes, and those that can result from the speculative power of modern credit markets.

In short, by combining MMT monetary sovereignty arguments with Minsky accounting and his core presentation of the financial instability hypothesis, Wray, Kelton and other MMTers apparently believe that they proposed program could not, per se, lead to financial instability problems. According to Tymoigne and Wray: "for financial fragility to increase, it has to be led by the private sector or governments that are not monetarily sovereign so that the move to Ponzi finance is possible. Economic growth, therefore, will not generate a weakening of the financial positions of private units if it is based on federal/ national government programs that continuously increase the surplus of the private sector and inject safe assets into the balance sheets of private units" (Tymoigne and Wray 2014, 28).

This lack of attention is more curious given Wray's and Tymoigne's discussion of the roots of the rise of "money manager capitalism," the great financial changes and dangerous financial innovations that contributed to the great financial crisis (see, for example, Tymoigne and Wray 2014, chaps. 2, 3, and 4).

So, they are surely aware of the speculative and dangerous activities of financial institutions as they search for yield and take on more risk using exotic financial innovations, associated with securitization. They refer to these dangers as processes of "layering" and pyramiding risk and leverage.[1] Yet they do not associate these possible problems as a possible outcome of their macroeconomic policies and that need attention.

6.4　Financial Speculation, Leverage and Asset Booms from Financialized Finance in the Context of MMT Macroeconomic Policy

There are several key flaws in this chain of reasoning. First of all, as Wry and Tymoigne recognize, there are other channels of financial instability despite the Minsky financial instability dynamic from hedge to speculative to ponzi financing.

More important, there have been the changes in modern financial markets, some of them recognized by MMTers themselves. The move to securitization, the increased role of swaps and derivatives; the layering and pyramiding of risks are all of critical importance. Crucially, these are facilitated by the use of collateral as a foundation for building these risky pyramids and creating these layers of leverage.

This key role of so-called "safe assets" in the creation of this collateral is important and often neglected (see McCauley 2019 and the large literature referenced there). When the US government runs budget deficits, it creates "safe" securities that play an important role not just in the US but also in the global financial system. Most analysts argue that these play a stabilizing role. But most of the literature neglects the fact that these assets form the foundation for collateral that global shadow banks, hedge funds, and other global financial institutions use to write swaps, derivatives, and make dangerous speculative bets. In short, in the modern globalized credit system, US government spending may increase the cash flow of private units, but it also creates financial assets that can promote more financial speculation and leverage.

---

[1] They note this as a part of the process of "financialization".

This problem goes on top of the problems Kindleberger and others point to with respect to long term low interest rates and their possible promotion of asset bubbles, leverage and excessive risk-taking.

In short, while US fiscal deficits combined with debt monetization at low interest rates might reduce speculative and ponzi financing through their cash flow impacts, the impacts through the "risk-taking" channel might make them much worse.

Part of the reason for MMTers lack of attention to channels such as these is their relative lack of attention to the growing role of shadow banking and their activities in the international arena. Without tracing this growth and seeing its connections to the key role of the dollar internationally, the possible financial instability problems associated with their proposed macroeconomic policies might not be easy for them to trace.

6.5 MMT Research on International Shadow Banking

Fortunately, some MMT analysts are exploring this global shadow banking system from an MMT perspective. Nersisyan and Dantas (2017), for example, note the major presence of global shadow banking, its role in creating global liquidity, and hint at the financial instability implications of this phenomenon. As MMTers themselves, they urge MMT analysts to explore this dimension further.

Such an exploration might also lead to an alteration of Wray's and other MMTers position on financial reform. Like many economists, they propose a strict set of regulations on deposit-taking banks, but more or less free reign for more risk-taking financial institutions, like nonbanks and hedge funds (see Tymoigne and Wray 2014, chap. 4). The growth of international shadow banking, as suggested by Nersisyan and Dantas, requires more attention to regulating these shadow banks, especially, I add, in the context of low interest rates, debt monetized, full employment fiscal policy by the United States.

6.6 Moving Forward

I have argued in this chapter that MMTers have ignored the possible Minskyesque financial dangers associated with their proposed macroeconomic policies because of their definitional and tautological arguments based on sovereign money and hedge financing, a narrow focus on the possible channels of financial instability, and a lack of attention to the global shadow finance mechanisms. As the work of Nersisyan and Dantas shows, there might be forward movement of MMT advocates to start adopting a more internationally oriented and more institutionally specific approach to the nature of the current global financial system. When they do, perhaps they will investigate the financial instability impacts of their proposed macroeconomic policy, and the domestic and international financial regulatory policies that would be useful in addressing these problems.

References

D'Arista, Jane. 2019. *All Fall Down*. Northampton: Edward Elgar.
Dymski, Gary, and Robert Pollin. 1992. "Hyman Minsky as Hedgehog: The Power of the Wall Street Paradigm." In *Financial Conditions and Macroeconomic Performance: Essays in Honor of Hyman P. Minsky*, edited by Steven Fazzari and Dimitri Papadimitriou, 27–62. Armonk: M.E. Sharpe.
Kindleberger, Charles P. 1978 and later editions. *Manias, Panics and Crashes*. New York: Basic Books.
McCauley, Robert N. 2019. "Safe Assets: Made, Not Just Born." BIS Working Paper, No. 769, Basel.
Minsky, Hyman. 1972. "Financial Instability Revisited: The Economics of Disaster." In *Reappraisal of the Federal Reserve Discount Mechanism*, edited by Board of Governors of the Federal Reserve System, 3: 95–136. Washington, DC: Board of Governors of the Federal Reserve System.
Minsky, Hyman. 1982. "The Financial-Instability Hypothesis: Capitalist Processes and the Behavior of the Economy." In *Financial Crises: Theory, History, and Policy*, edited by Charles P. Kindleberger and Jean-Pierre Laffargue, 13–39. New York: Cambridge University Press.
Minsky, Hyman. 1986. *Stabilizing an Unstable Economy*. New Haven: Yale University Press.
Nersisyan, Yeva, and Flavia Dantas. 2017. "Rethinking Liquidity Creation: Banks, Shadow Banks and the Elasticity of Finance." *Journal of Post Keynesian Economics* 40 (3): 279–299.
Tokunaga, Junji, and Gerald Epstein. 2018. "The Endogenous Finance of the Global Dollar-Based Financial System in the 2000s: A Minskian Approach." *Review of Keynesian Economics* 6 (1): 62–82.
Tymoigne, Eric. 2009. *Central Banking, Asset Prices and Financial Fragility*. New York: Routledge.
Tymoigne, Eric, and L. Randall Wray. 2014. *The Rise and Fall of Money Manager Capitalism: Minsky's Half Century from World War Two to the Great Recession*. 1st ed. (Critical Studies in Finance and Stability Book 3). Routledge: London.

CHAPTER 7

An MMT Free Lunch Mirage Can Lead to Perverse Outcomes: Fight Your Friends, Spare Your Enemies

Abstract Prominent Modern Money Theory (MMT) policy advocates often imply that progressive politicians do not need to discuss how to "pay for" important policy initiatives because sovereign money governments have no budget constraints. Some have even argued that discussing "paying for projects" is politically divisive. I argue the opposite. Implementing large programs like the Green New Deal (GND) would move the economy beyond full employment, requiring tax increases or spending cuts. Members of the progressive coalition supporting the policies would have to fight over who's policies get implemented. This chapter explores the implications of this political struggle and political problems such as these with MMT's approach. Some MMTers have only recently acknowledged that taxes or spending cuts would be needed to implement a GND.

Keywords Green New Deal · National priorities · Taxes

7.1 The Necessity of Trade-Offs and National Priority Setting for a Progressive Agenda, Even in an MMT World

A great appeal of Modern Money Theory (MMT) to some progressive politicians and activists (and to wealthy financiers as well) is that it appears to say: "We don't have to pay for government spending." Progressives who propose ambitious policy initiatives such as the "Green New Deal" (GND) proposed by Congresswoman Alexandria Ocasio-Cortez and Senator Ed Markey, are told by MMTers that they should simply argue for the desirability of these policies, and do not need to worry about how these initiatives are going to be "paid for." In response to claims from the austerity hawks that we cannot "afford" these proposals, the MMT answer is: by definition, we can always afford them because all we have to do is get the Fed to print dollars. In fact, they say, this happens virtually automatically anyway. And by the way, the US can never be forced to default, so this is not a big concern (see the MMT advocates quotes at the beginning of Chapter 2).[1]

How liberating and empowering this message is. But as I show in this chapter, this appearance of liberation and power is an illusion. Worse, it is a dangerous illusion.

The fundamental problem stems from a limitation that the MMT advocates themselves recognize. Even if there are no "financial limits" to deficit spending (a point which I address again later), there is a limit on the ability of the government simply to print money to finance government spending that the MMTers do recognize: this limit is full employment/full capacity utilization. Once full employment (or full capacity utilization) is reached, further demand for goods and service cannot be satisfied by new supply in the short term but must be provided by labor and production capacity that is already employed doing something else. Hence, the new government spending will necessarily "crowd out" the supply of other production, and if this spending is to be effectuated, this crowding out can be accompanied by increases in prices (inflation). At this point, there is no "free lunch," and all additional government spending has a "cost" in terms of other goods and services not being produced and possible further costs associated with high and increasing inflation if the policy is pushed too far.

---

[1] For example, see Kelton et al. (2018) on how to "pay for" the GND, written in November 2018: "the federal government can spend money on public priorities without raising revenue, and it won't wreck the nation's economy to do so. That may sound radical, but it's not. It's how the U.S. economy has been functioning for nearly half a century. That's the power of the public purse.... As a monopoly supplier of U.S. currency with full financial sovereignty, the federal government is not like a household or even a business. When Congress authorizes spending, it sets off a sequence of actions. Federal agencies, such as the Department of Defense or Department of Energy, enter into contracts and begin spending. As the checks go out, the government's bank — the Federal Reserve — clears the payments by crediting the seller's bank account with digital dollars. In other words, Congress can pass any budget it chooses, and our government already pays for everything by creating new money."

While some prominent MMT theorists and advocates such as Stephanie Kelton mention the need to make trade-offs at the point of full employment, the overwhelming message that MMT has repeatedly conveyed is that we don't need to worry about this because we can always "afford" to pay because we have "sovereign money." In a posting for Bloomberg News on February 1, 2019 entitled "*The Wealthy Are Victims of Their Own Propaganda to escape higher taxes, they must embrace deficits,*" Kelton ribs her wealthy friends who complain about progressive politicians like AOC and Elizabeth Warren's proposal for a new wealth tax. She tells them to get on board with MMT and stop worrying about budget deficits. MMT she tells them, means that, in all likelihood, no new taxes will be needed to pay for desirable new government spending proposals.

Understanding MMT, she says, will mean that people will be able to stop fighting about where the financing is going to come from. She chides these progressive politicians who have proposed new taxes to "pay for" their government spending initiatives:

> So that's why you see people like Representative Ocasio-Cortez and Senator Warren looking at the ultra-rich to fund their agendas. Billionaires are the magic money tree!

Kelton then calls for the MMT free lunch solution: monetize the expenditure without raising taxes. "Finally, consider what happens if we simply invest in programs to benefit the non-rich (student-debt forgiveness, free child care and so on) without treating the super-rich as our piggy bank.… It's sort of incredible that the option that is clearly better for *both* groups is the one we're most afraid of. But that's what happens when deficit phobias force politicians to 'pay for' everything by going where the money is" (Kelton 2019a).

Kelton does send a mixed message about the costs of the GND and related initiates. Around the same time, in an interview Kelton, says: "The way to approach a Green New Deal" GND is to adopt the method of economist John Maynard Keynes in his book How to Pay for the War: Model the economy's available resources; figure out what you can deploy and still avoid inflation; figure out how much private consumption spending you have to displace to make room for the necessary war spending; and finally, ensure a just transition, i.e., make sure that the poor and middle class, the ones deferring their private consumption spending, are rewarded for their sacrifice" (quoted in Roberts 2018).[2]

So, at the very best, MMT analysts are sending a mixed message to politicians and activists. The main message they convey in blogs, conferences and in the press has been that not only do we not need to ask how we are going to pay for programs but that to do so is divisive and counterproductive.

7.2 The MMT Free Lunch Illusion Leads to a Perverse Outcome: Fight Your Friends, Spare Your Enemies

Kelton claims that discussing how to pay for big initiatives like the GND will lead progressives to fight among each other and will prevent making progress on the profound problems facing us, like climate change

> The problem is that every politician is confronted with the question, 'How are you going to pay for it?' What these journalists are really asking is, 'Who's going to pay for it?' The question is designed to stop any meaningful policy debate *by dividing us up, and get us fighting over where the money is going to come from.* (italics added)

She goes on: "Since none of the headline politicians has really figured out how to respond—by explaining that when Congress approves a budget, the Treasury Department instructs the Federal Reserve to credit a seller's bank account—they all end up trying to answer it by pointing to some new revenue source" (Kelton 2019a).

Of course, I agree with Kelton and other MMTers that climate change is a profound threat and must be confronted.[3] But the refusal to discuss how to pay for massive programs like the proposed GND will have the opposite effect if, in fact, through the efforts of activists and progressive politicians we get close to passing legislation to implement these programs. Avoiding the discussion of who should bear the costs of these programs means that the wealthy and corporate interests will be left off the hook,

---

[2] See below, where I discuss Nersisyan and Wray's initial implementation of this approach, posted in May 2019 (Nersisyan and Wray 2019).

[3] See my discussion of climate change and colleagues Robert Pollin's and James Boyces' work on a program to confront it below.

and the progressives and their constituents will end up fighting each other over the available resources.

To see this, work through the following scenario. Let's say we have a coalition of various progressive groups that want to pass a large GND style policy into law, that includes the following set of programs[4]:

1. Employer of Last Resort Policy to guarantee full employment (a favorite policy of MMT advocates)
2. Addressing climate change[5]
3. Medicare for All[6] (note that this one may pay for itself)
4. Free (or debt free) college education
5. Universal Child Care

The illusion of empowerment that MMT seems to bring is that the coalition of forces that promotes these plans don't have to discuss who is going to pay for these programs. But going through a simple exercise shows that this is an illusion. If we implemented all these policies, then we would have "over" full employment. This is true almost by definition, in fact, because the Employer of Last Resort (ELR) policy creates full employment.[7] The GND plan itself also has a public job guarantee program. Even if we see these ELR programs as pulling people into the guaranteed jobs and then pushing them out as new, better jobs get created, somewhere along the line

---

[4] See the program of the "Green New Deal" https://ocasio-cortez.house.gov/sites/ocasio-cortez.house.gov/files/Resolution%20on%20a%20Green%20New%20Deal.pdf; Elizabeth Warren's "Universal Childcare Plan" https://www.vox.com/policy-and-politics/2019/2/22/18234606/warren-child-care-universal-2020 and the Employer of Last Resort plan, MMT's signature program for full employment (Tcherneva 2018).

[5] The GND as proposed by Ocasio-Cortez and Senator Markey itself contains many of these programs, including a public employment guarantee.

[6] As evaluated by Robert Pollin, this program more than pays for itself as far as the private economy is concerned but increases the costs to the government (Pollin et al. 2018).

[7] ELR proponents might point out that their program is like a "buffer stock" so that as job opportunities arise that pay better than the ELR, these workers would leave the ELR and be available to work elsewhere. But this point does not fundamentally alter the fact that somewhere along this group of policies, full capacity will be reached and, in anticipating that, all programs are on the "chopping bloc" of possibly pushing the economy past full capacity utilization. Hence, how to "pay for" the package through cuts elsewhere, increases in taxes, or pursuing policies that will increase capacity and productivity cannot be avoided (see Tcherneva 2018). Kelton ultimately confirmed this point (Kelton 2019b).

this group of programs will generate full employment and full capacity utilization as Wray has subsequently acknowledged (see below). Implementing the remaining programs will therefore create "over" full employment.

So, whichever programs get passed and implemented first will get a free ride under the "free lunch" MMT program. However, all the other programs will be abandoned unless their proponents can explain how the program will be paid for, by raising taxes or cutting spending elsewhere because implementing them will go beyond the full employment threshold. And by MMT logic, these would have to be "paid for."

In short, if the coalition does not find a way to "pay for" the group of programs as a whole, those that come up above the full employment line will have to be abandoned, or at least will have to come up with new taxes or spending cuts elsewhere to make the workers and capacity available to implement them. Who gets to go first is therefore crucial; or second; or third. Whose plan should get to go "scott free"? And whose plan will be on the chopping block?

In this world, the different members of the coalition will simply have to fight it out among themselves unless, they create the freed up production capacity in some other way: for example, by cutting government expenditure on less valuable or even destructive spending, such as the military, and or raise taxes to cut back consumption by those who already have too much.[8]

The important point is that, unless they are just going to fight it out amongst themselves to see who gets to go first, they will have to develop a *joint plan* to "pay for" their programs. MMT liberation from trade-offs and costs is an illusion.

One way to loosen this constraint is to focus spending on investment that creates more capacity. And indeed, this capacity expanding impact of new spending has long been a key consideration in assessing the desirability of different types of spending for heterodox economists and Keynes himself.[9] The phrase "spending on infrastructure will pay for itself" reflects this valid

---

[8]Dean Baker (2019) in a recent post argued that from a MMT perspective, high marginal tax rate programs like Ocasio-Cortez's is a bad idea because rich people don't have high marginal propensities to spend. So taxing them won't withdraw much aggregate demand. Mitchell (2018) made the same argument.

This is not a serious objection since in that case, they should be taxed even more. Dean Baker's related point about problems with tax evasion may be more valid (Baker 2019).

[9]When he wasn't making satirical points against the gold standard or "classical economics"—hence his tongue in cheek suggestions in the General Theory to build pyramids,

point that the supply side impacts of government spending are an important consideration in determining whether that type of spending can be fit in under the full employment-full capacity budget. Surprisingly, MMTers tend to greet such arguments with disdain because they imply a constraint on sovereign money governments.

In reality, we do have to engage in these "old" discussions of trade-offs and opportunity costs, investments vs. consumption—including supply-side impacts—even in a country with sovereign money and the world's premier international currency. The failure to acknowledge this leads to a completely perverse situation. By not talking about national priorities and cutting wasteful or destructive spending, progressives inadvertently give a pass to those who are wasting our resources or worse, using them in destructive ways. This means that we have to revive the discussions of national priorities; reducing the consumption capacity of the very rich (high marginal income taxes); tax reform, public investments, and the like. This is an old discussion; pre-MMT. Some might see this as "old hat" and obsolete in the world of modern money. But, in a successful policy regime that would bring us to full employment and possibly beyond, these costs and trade-offs need be emphasized from the outset in discussions of progressive macroeconomic policy, not brought in mostly as an after-thought.

7.3   MMT Acknowledges the Trade-Offs

Perhaps responding to criticisms such as these, very recently, Kelton, Wray, and some other MMT analysts have recognized that they could no longer avoid assessing the costs and trade-offs associated with a large government program such as the "Green New Deal" (Kelton, March 7, 2019b; Nersisyan and Wray, May 2019).[10]

Nersisyan and Wray's working paper, "How to Pay for the Green New Deal," acknowledges that the multipronged program is likely to bring the US economy beyond full employment and that, by the MMT's own "func-

---

churches, and put pound bills in bottles, bury them in the ground, and then dig them up, in order to generate employment.

[10] My Eastern Economics association paper, which is the precursor of this book, and contained this basic criticism, was circulated starting on February 27, 2019; an INET blog piece and a PERI Working Paper with this critique was posted March 20, 2019. Around the same time, other critics were questioning the MMT approach to the GND. Perhaps these criticisms led them to change their approach. Perhaps not.

tional finance" logic, this would require that aggregate demand be reduced elsewhere to allow resources to be moved toward the GND projects, and away from other uses. The methodology they use to estimate these costs and describe the program is based on and mimics that of J. M. Keynes's (1940) book, *How to Pay for the War: A Radical Plan for the Chancellor of the Exchequer* published in 1940.[11]

They use Keynes' approach for two main reasons: First, they argue that climate change represents a challenge at least as important as the challenges facing humanity in the great depression and the Second World War. And second, Keynes' approach focuses on the mobilization and reallocation of "real resources" and pierces the veil of the deficit and financing issues that are usually focused on in such discussions. Naturally, this focus on "real resources" fits the MMT approach, since they argue that financing with sovereign money is not an issue.

Nersisyan and Wray (2019) go through a number of estimates of the resource costs of the combination of most of the programs in the GND proposal including a public full employment program, a program to avoid catastrophic climate change, universal child care, and debt free public higher education. They focus not just on the resource costs of these programs, but also the ways in which these programs could provide real resources for each other. They thus attempt to asses a net resource utilization of these programs and compare that with estimates of the resource capacity of the US economy. This is a difficult task, and the results, as they describe, are only approximate and preliminary.

Their main results are as follows:

> This paper follows the methodology developed by J. M. Keynes in his *How to Pay for the War* pamphlet to estimate the "costs" of the Green New Deal (GND) in terms of resource requirements. Instead of simply adding up estimates of the government spending that would be required, we assess resource availability that can be devoted to implementing GND projects. This includes mobilizing unutilized and underutilized resources, as well as shifting resources from current destructive and inefficient uses to GND projects. We argue that financial affordability cannot be an issue for the sovereign US government. Rather, the problem will be inflation if sufficient resources cannot be diverted to the GND. And if inflation is likely, we need to put in place anti-inflationary measures, such as well-targeted taxes, wage and price

---

[11] Wray had referred to this methodology in the Roberts interview as noted above.

controls, rationing, and voluntary saving. Following Keynes, we recommend deferred consumption as our first choice should inflation pressures arise. We conclude that it is likely that the GND can be phased in without inflation, but if price pressures do appear, deferring a small amount of consumption will be sufficient to attenuate them. (p. 1)…Our main goal has been to set out a framework for analyzing the "cost" of the GND—not to promote any particular estimate of the "cost." ….We need an informed discussion of the best method of reducing resource use—should that become necessary—so as to free up resources for the GND. We have discussed deferred compensation as a preferred method. However, we believe that if the requirements turn out to be much larger than what we have estimated, we can also explore the other methods that were successfully used in WWII: patriotic saving (which is voluntary deferred consumption), price controls, rationing, and additional taxes. Most importantly, if taxes are to be used, they must be formulated to reduce resource use—not to "raise revenue." (p. 51)

This paper then is a recognition, despite previous claims to the contrary, that in fact, according to the logic of MMT itself, we need to talk about how to pay for a major program like the GND. Nersisyan and Wray bend over backwards to maintain the MMT terminology, as can be seen in the quote above: there is no need to "finance" the program; we do not need "to pay" for it, in a financial sense. They also try to limit the cost aspects by referring often to "deferred consumption" rather than taxes. In the end, though, they do clearly state that new taxes and perhaps other measures such as rationing, price controls, and so forth might be necessary. This might be the end of "free lunchism" for MMT and a very welcome change. Still, one wonders if this acknowledgement will make it into the blogs, political discussions and interviews. Some MMTers still insist that to bring up the need to "pay for" huge government programs, for example, by raising taxes, would be "divisive". Would it be more divisive than proposing price controls and rationing of the types FDR implemented during WWII after Pearl Harbor? Will MMTers acknowledge in these fora that these are their plan B policies if the economy overheats?

Though acknowledging the possible trade-offs is a step forward for MMT, it is important to note the limitations of this approach. I will not go into an assessment of their particular estimates or program for "paying" for the GND. But there are a few points relevant to the focus of the book. Nersisyan and Wray avoid all explicit discussion of the financial side of conducting a major government program like the GND. They assume that if there is a major government deficit, it will be financed by the Federal

Reserve and that will be the end of the financial story. But things might not be so simple. It would be necessary to analyze the amount of debt or debt monetization that would be required and what the impacts of this would be on the US and global economy. These impacts might be relatively small. Taylor (2019), for example, thinks these could be substantial.

Though the analogy is very far from perfect, since Nersisyan and Wray used the UK war finance as an example, it is worth noting that Great Britain ended up with a massive war debt to the United States following the Second World War. Whereas going into the War, the UK was still a major reserve currency country, by the end, its status had been greatly diminished.

Of course, the situation of the United States and the war against climate change is completely different. The dollar is still the premier reserve currency, and this is unlikely to dramatically change due only from a sensibly implemented GND program. Still, financial implications cannot be ignored in these scenarios.

Though I will not focus on this here, it is clear that the "How to Pay for the Green New Deal paper" fails to address the policy tools that have been developed over many years to deal with the fight against climate change: Cap and Dividend approaches (Boyce 2019), carbon taxes, government subsidies and the like (Pollin et al. 2014; Pollin 2015. Also, see Chapter 8 in this book).

Nonetheless, the paper represents an MMT step forward in confronting a more realistic, institutionally based and politically transparent analysis of macroeconomic policy options.

References

Baker, Dean. 2019. "MMT and Taxing the Rich." CEPR, February 15.
Boyce, James K. 2019. *The Case for Carbon Dividends*. London: Polity Press.
Kelton, Stephanie. 2019a. "The Wealthy Are Victims of Their Own Propaganda." Bloomberg. Accessed June 15, 2019.
Kelton, Stephanie. 2019b. "How to Tell When Deficit Spending Crosses a Line." Bloomberg, March 7.
Kelton, Stephanie, Andres Bernal, Greg Carlock, and Guest Writers. 2018. "Opinion | We Can Pay for a Green New Deal." HuffPost, November 30. https://www.huffpost.com/entry/opinion-green-new-deal-cost_n_5c0042b2e4b027f1097bda5b.
Keynes, John Maynard. 1940. *How to Pay for the War: A Radical Plan for the Chancellor of the Exchequer*. New York: Harcourt, Brace.

Mitchell, Bill. 2018. "The 'Tax the Rich' Call Bestows Unwarranted Importance on them." Modern Monetary Theory Blog, February 21.
Nersisyan, Yeva, and L. Randall Wray. 2019. "How to Pay for the Green New Deal." *SSRN Scholarly Paper ID 3398983*. Rochester, NY: Social Science Research Network. https://papers.ssrn.com/abstract=3398983.
Pollin, Robert. 2015. *Greening the Global Economy*. Cambridge: MIT Press.
Pollin, Robert, Heidi Garrett-Peltier, James Heintz, and Bracken Hendricks. 2014. "Green Growth: A U.S. Program for Controlling Climate Change and Expanding Job Opportunities." Political Economy Research Institute.
Pollin, Robert, James Heintz, Peter Arno, Jeannette Wicks-Lim, and Michael Ash. 2018. "Economic Analysis of Medicare for All." Political Economy Research Institute (PERI), November.
Roberts, David. 2018. "The Green New Deal, Explained." Vox, December 21. https://www.vox.com/energy-and-environment/2018/12/21/18144138/green-new-deal-alexandria-ocasio-cortez.
Taylor, Lance. 2019. "Macroeconomic Stimulus à la MMT." INET. https://www.ineteconomics.org/perspectives/blog/macroeconomic-stimulus-%C3%A0-la-mmt.
Tcherneva, Pavlina. 2018. "The Job Guarantee: Design, Jobs, and Implementation." *SSRN Electronic Journal*.

CHAPTER 8

Conclusion: Contours of a Progressive Macroeconomic Policy

Abstract This concluding chapter summarizes the main arguments of *What's Wrong with Modern Money Theory?* I argue that while I share many of the policy goals of MMT advocates, I have some significant concerns about the arguments and evidence for their proposals, and the likely feasibility and impacts of them, especially world-wide. To illustrate that better approaches do exist, I present an extended example of research PERI economists have done on an "employment targeted" macroeconomic policy for South Africa. I also briefly discuss work that PERI economists have done on programs to mitigate climate change. I discuss these in the spirit of promoting more programmatic discussions among progressive economists with similar policy goals.

Keywords Employment targeting · Green transition · Cap and dividend

8.1 INTRODUCTION

Modern Money Theory (MMT) has gained a great deal of attention in the last several years, largely because of its persistent criticism of simple-minded, and destructive austerity arguments and demands from neo-liberal economists and politicians in the United States, Europe and elsewhere. More recently, prominent MMT advocates such as Stephanie Kelton and Randall Wray have gained additional interest because of their arguments

© The Author(s) 2019
G. A. Epstein, *What's Wrong with Modern Money Theory?*,
https://doi.org/10.1007/978-3-030-26504-5_8

supporting the financial affordability of progressive policy ideas, such as the "Green New Deal." MMT's persistent criticism of wrong-headed austerity economics, along with the long-standing arguments and efforts of other heterodox economists (see, for example, Baker et al. 1998; Palley 2000; Galbraith 2008; Pollin 2012; Blyth 2013; Crotty 2012; Herndon et al. 2014), has helped to shift the debate on austerity and budget deficits, in many respects in a positive direction. MMT's, along with other heterodox economists' efforts, in that respect, should be applauded.

MMT advocates' effective use of blogs and social media as well as networking has been particularly effective in generating discussion about these issues. As this book shows, while I am quite critical of the approach and particular arguments that MMT analysts use to fight against austerity economics, I am very supportive of many of their goals in this respect.

In fact, I wrote this book because I am concerned that some of the arguments MMT advocates use, the way they use them and some key aspects of their underlying theory and approach have some severe problems. I care about this because I fear that, even though many of their goals might be ones I share, some aspects of their approach will ultimately undermine the achievement of those goals.

In this concluding chapter, I first summarize the key arguments I have made in *What's Wrong with Modern Money Theory?* And then I conclude with a very brief discussion of examples of what I consider to be some better approaches to doing macroeconomic policy analysis from a progressive perspective.

8.2 Summary of Main Conclusions

In *What's Wrong with Modern Money Theory? A Policy Critique* I have focused on one key part of the MMT approach: its policy proposals for fiscal and monetary policy and the underlying arguments MMT analysts present in support of these policy proposals. My book differs from many other critiques of MMT because its main concern is macroeconomic policy, not theory. Of course, since MMT's policy approach is grounded in some of their key theories, then theoretical issues arise in so far as they relate to the policy issues.

My major theoretical complaint is that, on matters related to MMT monetary and fiscal policy, they rely excessively on definitional and tautological defenses of their claims about the impacts of these policies. Many of these defenses are based on their definition of "sovereign money" and their focus

8 CONCLUSION: CONTOURS OF A PROGRESSIVE MACROECONOMIC POLICY

on short-run automatic impacts rather than longer term effects. Examples are their ignoring possible financial instability problems associated with government spending largely because their claim that these problems are ruled out by definition for "sovereign money" countries; and their claim that more government spending lowers interest rates, simply because this might be the short-run quasi-automatic impact of more spending on the policy rate, rather than the more important medium to longer run impacts due to discretionary changes in monetary policy and the reactions of the financial markets. This focus on definitional and tautological argumentation leads to my main policy critiques. My major critique of MMT's policy approach is that its advocates pay too little attention to empirical evidence, and, in some important regards, institutional specificity and hierarchies of power. These criticisms overlap in what I call the "mystery of the missing Minsky" in Chapter 6: MMTers paradoxical lack of attention in the context of their proposals concerning monetary and fiscal policy to domestic and especially global credit dynamics and the potential of these dynamics to produce financial instability and crisis. This is a paradox because MMT analysts are close students of Minsky's writings, and many write extensively about his work.

I argue that these problems lead to several key limitations and flaws in MMT's arguments that undermine the general validity of their policy proposals.

In these pages, I have tried to address some obvious questions about the viability of MMT proposed macro-policies: what would be their impacts on inflation, exchange rate instability, interest rates, financial instability, investment and economic growth? What, ultimately, are the limits and constraints on MMT macro policy? Discussing the institutional limits of this approach, the lack of supportive empirical evidence for some of their key arguments, and the potentially politically dangerous policy arguments they have made in support of some of their perspectives on debt accumulation and monetary policy, have formed the core of *What's Wrong with Modern Money Theory?*

My main conclusions in the book are as follows:

First, even though MMT advocates claim that their macroeconomic framework applies to all countries with "sovereign currencies," there is significant evidence that it does not apply to the vast majority of countries in the developing world that are integrated into global financial markets. As is well-known, these countries are subject to the vagaries of international capital flows, sometimes called "sudden stops." The problem is that in light of these flows, these countries have limited fiscal and monetary policy space, surely insufficient to conduct MMT prescribed monetary and fiscal policies for full employment. Randall Wray argues that flexible exchange rates are sufficient to provide sufficient policy space for these countries to undertake MMT macro-policies. Occasionally the issue of capital controls is briefly mentioned, especially by William Mitchell, but few MMT analysts make this a key part of their argument. Contrary to the MMT view, a careful survey of the empirical evidence casts grave doubts on the effectiveness of flexible rates for giving policy autonomy or insulating these countries from the vagaries of global financial flows. This problem is worse for countries that cannot borrow in their own currencies, but also applies to small open countries that are able to borrow in their own currencies and therefore have a larger degree of monetary *sovereignty*. The upshot is that only countries that issue their own internationally accepted currency ("hard currency") *might* have the policy space to conduct MMT policies.

Second, even for those countries that issue their own international currencies, the sustainability and "exploitability" of the international role is not absolute. The country that has the greatest fiscal and monetary space is the United States, which issues the predominant key currency, the US dollar. Whereas Wray has written confidently that the predominance of the dollar is not something we will need to worry about in our lifetime, historical and empirical evidence suggests that even considerable forces for persistence of key currency positions can weaken over time, perhaps even fall rapidly and dramatically. This is especially true when there are competing currencies with both a "will" and a "way" to achieve key currency status. China (and to a lesser extent, the Eurozone) are competitors in this sense. There is significant evidence of a move to a multicurrency system in which dollar holders can more easily switch out of the dollar if significant, perceived problems arise, such as high exchange rate instability, or excessive inflation. In such a world, the ability of the US government to exploit the dollar's "exorbitant privilege" to sustain very large debt levels or sustained low interest rates will most likely have limits. To be sure, these limits are uncertain, but history suggests that the US cannot completely ignore them.

Third, even if the dollar's role continues indefinitely to create space to implement MMT macro-policies, that doesn't mean that the US should actually do so. MMT proposed policy amounts to an "America First" macroeconomic policy. While it is traditional for the US (and other countries) to ignore the impacts of their macroeconomic policies on the rest of the world, presumably a progressive approach to policy would adopt a more internationalist perspective. There is significant evidence that there are substantial spillover effects of US monetary policy on emerging market and developing countries that are transmitted largely through the dollar's predominant international role. These spillover effects can be highly destabilizing if the Federal Reserve pursues excessively loose or tight monetary policy—without any consideration of their impacts on developing countries. For example, as D'Arista (2019) shows, the low interest rates of the Greenspan era helped to generate dangerous levels of dollar-denominated leverage in emerging markets which contributed to the spread of financial crisis in 2007–2008. A more internationalist, progressive approach to macroeconomic would take these impacts into account.

A fourth point concerns the issue of financial instability. MMT advocates might argue that their proposed low US interest rates would facilitate growth in developing countries by reducing the cost of capital for these countries so that the spillovers would be good, not bad. But by itself, this claim ignores the highly speculative nature of modern international financial markets. A careful analysis of the impact of low, long term interest rates by the key currency country, the US, shows that in the absence of strong financial regulations domestically and internationally, the impact is likely to be the accumulation of high leverage, asset bubbles and financial instability. Yet MMT theorists talk very little in the context of their proposed macroeconomic policies about the necessary role of financial regulations and capital account regulations in channeling funds productively and limiting financial crises. This is puzzling in view of their long association with the work of Hyman Minsky. In short, this relative lack of attention to financial instability and broad-based financial regulation in the context of their proposed monetary and fiscal policy is a key example of their inattention to institutional and empirical constraints on the policies they propose and, in my view, a significant flaw in their macroeconomic policy approach.[1]

Fifth, much of MMT's policy appeal stems from the perception that the theory implies that progressives with programmatic plans do not need to

---

[1] As I argue in Chapter 6, MMT analysts do, of course, discuss financial regulations. In fact, some MMT advocates, including William Black, are experts and prolific writers on the topic. But in the context of their macroeconomic policy proposals, the discussion of financial regulation is quite limited. And where it exists, it focuses on regulating primarily banks, and not hedge funds and other "shadow banking" institutions. This is quite problematic in a world where these financial institutions have become so important in the global economy and to the state of financial stability.

talk or worry about the costs of these programs or how they are going to be "paid for." But even within the framework of MMT itself, this claim of a free lunch is incorrect. Recall that MMT theorists recognize that at or around full employment, further economic expansion could lead to an increase in inflation and if this fiscal and monetary expansion were pushed too far, inflation could accelerate. In this world, at full employment, the government would have to raise taxes or cut private or other public spending in order to make room for new fiscal initiatives. This is no free lunch.

It would be better to recognize at the outset that there is no free lunch as the economy moves toward full employment. It would be better to engage in the old-fashioned exercise of arguing for national priorities and discussing taxes. To free up production capacity in a progressive way, rather than cut the progressive policies, it would be better, for example, to cut excessive government military expenditures, and raise taxes on the wealthy and others, if necessary. This means that policy advocates do have to discuss from the beginning national priorities, taxes, and means to "pay for programs," even within the narrow confines of MMT. The failure to do so leads to a completely perverse situation that spares the progressive's enemies and gores their allies. After years of mainly denying this, Wray and Nersisyan's recent paper on "How to Pay for the Green New Deal" is a recognition of this and an important step in the direction of a realistic analysis of macroeconomic policy trade-offs. One hopes that MMT analysts do more macroeconomic policy work in this vein.[2]

But here, again, the institutional context is important. Nersisyan's and Wray's policy proposals to create the capacity to implement a GND rely heavily on the types of state-directed resource allocation policies used during the New Deal and Second World War in the US and the Second World War. Their program is thus reliant on policies such as price controls and rationing, "voluntary saving" and "deferred consumption." It is important to note that addressing climate change is a two or three-decades-long project, or longer. Are these types of programs feasible, or even desirable in twenty-first-century US on such a long-term basis?

In short, once one acknowledges that trade-offs may exist and detailed macroeconomic policies will be necessary to overcome these trade-offs, the work of designing institutionally relevant and feasible macroeconomic policies will be required. MMT advocates have undertaken this type of

---

[2] MMT analysts have done a good deal of concrete, institutionally based work on their employer of last resort proposals (see, for example, Tcherneva 2018; Wray et al. 2018).

work with their arguments for public employment programs, but have less experience doing it in other realms, presumably because they have mostly focused on their arguments that such trade-offs are not necessary.

8.3 Institutionally Grounded and Empirically Based Progressive Macroeconomic Policy: A Few Examples

Fortunately, other heterodox economists have been undertaking institutionally specific, empirically based studies of macroeconomics and related areas such as climate policy, for a number of years. Here I mention just a few examples out of many possible candidates.

For example, in 2005–2006, a team of colleagues led by Robert Pollin, in which I participated developed for the United Nations Development Program an employment targeted macroeconomic policy strategy for South Africa, a country that at that time had an unemployment rate well above 20% (Pollin et al. 2006). The goal of the study was to design an integrated macroeconomic program that could halve the unemployment rate within ten years, and that would be consistent with important macroeconomic policy constraints faced by the South African economy. The strategy was also designed to build on the macroeconomic institutions already in place and policy tools that seemed feasible within the period of time available. Still, the approach pushed many boundaries and was designed to be transformative at the same time.

Pollin et al. proposed an integrated set of policies that included expanded direct government spending, increased subsidies for labor-intensive sectors, an expansion of public works employment schemes. To move credit toward the favored sectors, increased use of the existing network of development banks, loan guarantees, and asset-based reserve requirements were proposed. We proposed that the Reserve Bank of South Africa support these schemes with their monetary and credit policies, while lending administrative support.

To confront the constraints and trade-offs that the South African economy faced, including the possibility of capital flight, exchange rate and inflation pressures, and international borrowing constraints, Pollin et al. proposed an integrated series of policies including increasing government borrowing, increases in taxes, capital controls, and the promotion of more competition in key price-setting industries that were beset with monopoly inefficiencies and rents.

To develop the program and determine the macroeconomic impacts, the team utilized a variety of analytical techniques including input–output analysis, macroeconometric modeling, sectoral analyses, and qualitative analysis based on interviews and site visits. We also draw on a long-standing body of work that included analysis of capital controls, developmental banking, alternatives to inflation targeting monetary policy, fiscal policy and employment issues.[3]

In the end, unfortunately, our proposals were not accepted by the government and so their impact on the actual policy was minimal, to none. Unemployment remains unacceptably high in South Africa today. But I briefly discuss this report because it represents the kind of institutionally based, empirically grounded, and financially integrated study that takes into account realistic assessments of constraints and trade-offs in the analysis of major economic programs. Other heterodox economists have developed many other such programs over the years, including Keith Griffin 1999, and Lance Taylor and his students (see, for example, Ocampo et al. 2009).

8.4 Confronting Climate Change

My colleagues at PERI, especially Robert Pollin and James Boyce and their associates have undertaken numerous detailed studies of the benefits, employment creation, costs, and mechanisms for achieving a sustainable, green energy future, for the US, for several US states, and for numerous countries around the world (see the work at PERI, especially, Pollin et al. 2014, 2015; Pollin 2015, 2017; Boyce 2019).[4]

Pollin's research has included various taxation and other financing/incentive programs to facilitate the redirection of investment toward renewable energy and conservation. James Boyce has studied the impacts of "cap and dividend" policies to set caps on greenhouse gas emissions while utilizing the revenues from auctioning off carbon permits to rebate income and to finance government programs to promote climate change. The institutionally grounded, empirically based and detailed approaches contained in these studies are examples of the kind of work necessary to make progress on solving this existential threat. Their work has been imple-

---

[3] See, for example, Epstein et al. (2003), Epstein (2007), Epstein and Yeldan (2009), and Pollin (2012), and of course, much other work by heterodox economists.

[4] See, PERI's program on Environmental and Energy Economics (https://www.peri.umass.edu/research-areas/environmental-andenergy-economics).

mented in President Obama's "stimulus" program after the great financial crisis (Pollin et al. 2014) and various climate bills put forward in Congress (Boyce 2019). Of course, many others are doing this kind of work as well.

8.5 FINAL REMARKS

Despite my critiques of MMT detailed in this book, it is important to remember that MMT's approach to assessing the costs and benefits of the GND and their earlier work on employment guarantees offer some important insights in how to conceptualize these issues, including their utilization of ideas from functional finance, and their focus on debt monetization as a useful complementary tool to use in these programs. MMT's warnings against the dangerous focus on austerity and of the dangers of the structure of the Euro System have also played an important role in recent years. These examples and the examples of policy initiatives discussed in this chapter suggests that we do have ideas to learn from each other.

Moving forward, if we are going to solve the profound problems facing our country and the world, such as addressing the climate crisis, achieving full employment and greater equality, and providing decent health care for all, a more constructive dialogue among economists and policy analysts trying to achieve similar goals would be a very positive step.

REFERENCES

Baker, Dean, Gerald Epstein, and Robert Pollin (eds.). 1998. *Globalization and Progressive Economic Policy*. Cambridge and New York: Cambridge University Press.
Blyth, Mark. 2013. *Austerity: The History of a Dangerous Idea*. Oxford and New York: Oxford University Press.
Boyce, James K. 2019. *The Case for Carbon Dividends*. London: Polity Press.
Crotty, James. 2012. "The Great Austerity War: What Caused the US Deficit Crisis and Who Should Pay to Fix It?" *Cambridge Journal of Economics* 36 (1): 79–104.
D'Arista, Jane. 2019. *All Fall Down*. Northampton, MA: Edward Elgar.
Epstein, Gerald. 2007. "Central Banks as Agents of Economic Development." In *Institutional Change and Economic Development*, edited by Ha-Joon Chang. New York: United Nations University; London: Anthem Press; Reprinted in Gerald Epstein, *The Political Economy of Central Banking: Contested Control and the Power of Finance*. Northampton, MA: Edward Elgar, 2019.

Epstein, Gerald, Ilene Grabel, and Jomo K. S. 2003. "Capital Management Techniques in Developing Countries." In *Challenges to the World Bank and IMF; Developing Country Perspectives*, edited by Ariel Buira. London: Anthem Press.

Epstein, Gerald, and Erinc Yeldan, eds. 2009. *Beyond Inflation Targeting: Monetary Policy for Employment Generation and Poverty Reduction*. Northampton, MA: Edward Elgar Press.

Galbraith, James. 2008. *The Predator State: How Conservatives Abandoned the Free Market and Why Liberals Should Too*. New York: The Free Press.

Griffin, Keith. 1999. *Alternative Strategies for Economic Development*. New York: Palgrave Macmillan.

Herndon, Thomas, Michael Ash, and Robert Pollin. 2014. "Does High Public Debt Consistently Stifle Economic Growth? A Critique of Reinhart and Rogoff." *Cambridge Journal of Economics* 38 (2): 257–279.

Ocampo, José Antonio, Codrina Rada, and Lance Taylor. 2009. *Growth and Policy in Developing Countries: A Structuralist Approach*. Initiative for Policy Dialogue at Columbia University. New York: Columbia University Press.

Palley, Thomas. 2000. *Plenty of Nothing the Downsizing of the American Dream and the Case for Structural Keynesianism*. Princeton: Princeton University Press.

Pollin, Robert. 2012. *Back to Full Employment*. Cambridge: MIT Press.

Pollin, Robert. 2015. *Greening the Global Economy*. Cambridge: MIT Press.

Pollin, Robert. 2017. *Global Green Growth for Human Development*. New York: Human Development Program.

Pollin, Robert, Gerald Epstein, James Heintz, and Leonce Ndikumana. 2006. *An Employment-Targeted Economic Program for South Africa*. Northampton, MA: Edward Elgar.

Pollin, Robert, Heidi Garrett-Peltier, James Heintz, and Bracken Hendricks. 2014. *Green Growth: A U.S. Program for Controlling Climate Change and Expanding Job Opportunities*. Amherst, MA: Political Economy Research Institute.

Pollin, Robert, Heidi Garrett-Peltier, James Heintz, and Shouvik Chakraborty. 2015. *Global Green Growth: Clean Energy Industrial Investments and Expanding Job Opportunities*. Amherst, MA: Political Economy Research Institute.

Tcherneva, Pavlina R. 2018. "The Job Guarantee: Design, Jobs, and Implementation." *SSRN Electronic Journal*.

Wray, L. R., F. Dantas, S. Fullwiler, P. R. Tcherneva, and S. A. Kelton. 2018. "Public Service Employment: A Path to Full Employment." Research Project Report. Annandale-on-Hudson, NY: Levy Economics Institute of Bard College, April.

Index

A
Asset bubbles, 9, 13, 24, 29, 61, 66, 71, 74, 93
Austerity, 2–4, 8, 23, 28, 30, 78, 89, 90, 97

B
Bretton Woods, 48

C
Capital controls/capital account regulations/macro-prudential regulations, 9, 11–13, 24, 36, 40, 41, 45, 62, 66, 92, 93, 95, 96
Central bank, 5, 18–20, 22–24, 26–28, 30, 36, 47, 62
Central bank independence, 2, 23, 50, 51
Chartalism, 19–21
China, 12, 51–54, 92
Credit, 5, 7–10, 18, 21, 23, 24, 30, 39, 59–62, 66, 73, 80, 91, 95
Currency zones, 52, 53

Current account/current account deficit, 37, 46, 49, 53

D
Debt monetization, 5, 23, 26, 50, 67, 74, 86, 97
Developing countries/emerging market economies/Global South, 9, 11–13, 27, 30, 31, 35–39, 41, 45, 46, 58–62, 66, 93

E
Emerging markets, 12, 39, 41, 59, 60, 66, 93
Employer of Last Resort, 81. *See also* Public employment programs
Endogenous money, 19, 22
Euro/Eurozone, 10, 12, 37, 38, 47, 48, 53, 54, 92
Exorbitant privilege/dollar's hegemony, 12, 48, 54, 57, 62, 92

F

Federal Reserve, 2, 5, 12, 18, 22, 23, 26, 28, 46, 49, 58–60, 65, 78, 80, 86, 93
Financial instability/financial speculation/financial bubbles, 10, 13, 24, 26, 29, 36, 60, 61, 66, 67, 69, 71, 72, 74, 75, 91, 93
Financial instability hypothesis, 66, 69, 72
Financial regulations, 5, 8, 12, 13, 24, 62, 66, 93
Fine tuning, 21, 25, 61
Fiscal policy, 4–6, 10, 11, 13, 20, 21, 24, 25, 28–30, 39, 60, 61, 67, 71, 74, 91–93, 96
Fiscal space, 36, 37
Flexible exchange rate, 11, 31, 36, 39, 40, 45, 92
exchange rate instability, 10, 12, 37, 91, 92
Full capacity, 5, 78, 81–83
Full employment, 2, 4–7, 9, 11, 13, 19, 20, 24, 25, 28–30, 36, 37, 40, 41, 47, 57, 60, 61, 66, 71, 74, 78, 79, 81–84, 92, 94, 97
Functional finance, 5, 6, 19, 25, 29, 30, 84, 97

G

Global Financial Crisis/Great Financial Crisis, 2, 53, 54, 72, 97
Green energy/renewable energy, 96
Green New Deal (GND), 5, 13, 78–81, 83–86, 90, 94, 97

H

Hedge/speculative/ponzi scheme, 6, 7, 9, 24, 66, 68, 70–74, 93
Hot money flows/capital inflows, 66

I

Inflation, 2, 5–7, 9–13, 19, 25, 28–30, 46, 50, 51, 53, 54, 61, 65, 78, 79, 84, 85, 91, 92, 94–96

L

Low interest rates, 9, 12, 24, 28–30, 39, 46, 49, 57, 61, 62, 66, 71, 74, 92, 93

M

Minsky, Hyman, 5, 13, 19, 66, 67, 93
Modern Money Theory (MMT), 1–13, 18–31, 35, 36, 39–41, 45–50, 53, 54, 57, 58, 60–62, 65–67, 71, 72, 74, 75, 78–86, 89–94, 97
Monetary policy/spillovers of the US monetary policy, 5, 6, 9, 11, 12, 21, 23, 25, 28, 29, 31, 37, 46, 50, 58–62, 90–93, 96
Monetary sovereignty, 20, 47, 72, 92

P

Political Economy Research Institute (PERI), 83, 96
Post-Keynesian, 1, 4, 7, 18, 19, 21–23
Property rights, 50, 52
Public debt, 20, 27, 28, 66
Public employment programs, 20, 81, 95, 97

R

Renminbi, 47, 48, 54
Reserve currency/global currency/hard currencies/key currency, 11, 12, 41, 46, 47, 49–54, 86, 92, 93

S

Safe heaven, 48
Shadow banking, 9, 67, 74, 93
Soft currency, 47
Sudden stop, 36, 37, 59

T

Tobin Tax, 62